MOOSE On The LOOSE

True Tales to make you Laugh, Chortle, Snicker and Feel Inspired

Edited by Matt Jackson

Summit Studios

Library and Archives Canada Cataloguing in Publication

Moose on the loose : true tales to make you laugh, chortle, snicker, and feel inspired / edited by Matt Jackson.

Issued also in an electronic format.
ISBN 978-0-9866856-0-6

1. Outdoor life–Canada--Humor. 2. Voyages and travels–Humor. 3. Canadian wit and humor (English). I. Jackson, Matt

PN6178.C3M667 2012   796.50971   C2012-904548-9

Designed by Kirk Seton, Signet Design Inc.
Cover Photo by Doug Lindstrand
Printed and bound in Canada

SUMMIT STUDIOS
80 Cardinal Cres.
Newmarket, Ontario
L3Y 5Y4 Canada

This book is dedicated to all travelers who

venture forth bravely and come home

with stories to share

Table of Contents

Introduction   1
Matt Jackson

Summer of the Lost Ham   5
Laurie Gough

Hiking the Alps in Flip-flops   13
Ryan Clement

Moose on the Loose   24
Sylvia Shawcross

One Little Ounce   35
Barbara McAlear

Monkey Business   38
Rita Pomade

Dinner with Nine Men   46
Angela Goodman

Adventures with Reverend Lugio   52
Brent Curry

The Turkish Bath   70
Heather Lea

Purple and Green   74
Matt Hill

Jumping the Bull
Maureen Magee — 85

Four Dollars and a Microwave
Kyle MacDonald — 90

Cornbread and Wolverines
Tim Irvin — 98

Yoga Matt
Kelly Kittel — 103

Tarzan
Natasha Deen — 109

Snooper
Sterling Haynes — 117

Lake Expectations
Philip Torrens — 121

Hillbillies
Sylvia Fleming — 129

Ten Thousand Cows
Tim Tentcher — 135

Adventures in Moving
Alice Newton — 140

Charming
Stuart Reininger

147

What's in a Name?
Karen Paquin

155

Leave 'Em at Home
Maureen Magee

160

Traveling Light is for Schmucks
Colleen Friesen

169

Chaos Theory
Brent Curry

174

Hell No Longer on Wheels
Rebecca Berry

182

Critters in the Pool
Doug Underhill

192

All is Well
B.A. Markus

200

Acknowledgements

218

Introduction

By Matt Jackson

Over the last few years I've edited six travel and outdoor humor anthologies. During that time I've "discovered" some incredible storytellers, a few of whom have gone on to accomplish much greater things in the world of travel literature.

Kyle MacDonald, for example, after we published his first ever story in *I Sold My Gold Tooth for Gas Money* (2006), managed to trade a red paperclip into progressively more valuable items until he had a house. The book that he wrote about that adventure—titled *One Red Paperclip*—was published by Random House a year later, and has received a great deal of international acclaim. More recently, fan favorite Conor Grennan—who has contributed several popular stories to our anthology series—had his travel memoir *Little Princes* published by HarperCollins. The book describes his time working at a Nepalese orphanage, after which he was inspired to set up an organization to help reunite displaced children with their parents.

It is always heartening to see a contributor move on to greater things as a writer, and it makes me wonder who among our stable of *Moose on the Loose* scribes will chisel out a more prominent role for themselves on the writing stage. Maureen Magee comes to mind. It's not that Magee has never been published, it's just that in my opinion she should have a broader audience considering her talents. Not only did she win the Grand Prize in this year's Summit Studios story contest, but she managed to place *two* stories in this anthology. "Jumping the Bull" is a classic yarn of the "Lost in Translation" persuasion, where she is forced to respond to a marriage proposal from a stranger while working on an African film set. "Leave 'Em at Home" is an ode to the tribulations of traveling with a longtime friend who happens to have far different tastes.

Another writer who stands out is Ryan Clement from Brandon, Manitoba—also a prizewinner from this year's story contest. Clement has a keen eye for detail, and a knack for seeing humor in what to many would be small and insignificant details. His story "Hiking the Alps in Flip-flops" would have fallen flat with a lesser talent, but Clement's take on his "Swiss incident" kept both myself and the rest of the contest judges in stitches.

There are also a few veteran travel writers who've contributed to this book. One of them is Laurie Gough, who shares her tale of paddling the mighty Yukon River in "Summer of the Lost Ham." In this tale she describes with juicy details her encounter with one of the most memorable characters that I've ever read about in travel literature. For anybody who has read Bill Bryson's *A Walk in the Woods*, think: male version of Mary Ellen.

Another of my favorite stories was penned by seasoned scribe Colleen Friesen and is titled, "Traveling Light is for Schmucks." It wouldn't be a collection of funny stories without a generous helping of self-deprecation in a few of them, and Friesen takes that creed to new levels while having a heck of a good time along the way.

One would think that as an editor of travel anthologies I would have read it all, but I'm happy to report that is not the case. I'm often surprised by the freshly original stories I receive from would-be contributors. Some writers still manage to catch me off-guard. Case in point: one of the most unexpected stories I encountered was "Adventures with Reverend Lugio," which was written by Brent Curry. It plays off a theme that anybody who has spent time on the Internet has encountered at some point: that of fraudsters trying to scam you out of your money by way of numerous shady propositions. In this case, however, Curry turns the tables on the would-be scam artists and manages to have a remarkable adventure along the way.

And what of the title track you might ask? Is this book about Moose? On the Loose? Well, no. Not really. You've probably guessed that already. The stories are much too diverse for that. As with previous Summit Studios anthologies, I've found one story in the mix that I felt would translate well into a book title. In this particular case the story was written by Sylvia Shawcross of Gatineau, Quebec, a writer whom the legendary Farley Mowat describes as "a rarity of our times, an honest to goodness satirist."

I first heard about this particular story when Shawcross made an offhand comment to me during an email exchange, and it was so tantalizing that I practically begged her to write it up. It features the unbelievable story of Shawcross and her family driving across Canada with a gigantic moose head (wrapped in a polka dot tablecloth, no less) strapped to the top of their van. She was a little girl at the time. Add to this the chicanery of her father, who began making up all kinds of stories about the moose as they traveled from one province to the next. By the time they had reached Saskatchewan the stories had become so outlandish that Shawcross's mother—worried that he was setting a bad example for *his* children—was threatening rebellion.

I hope you enjoy reading this collection of stories as much as I've enjoyed editing it. Moreover, if you have a funny story of your own, I hope you'll consider sending it to us so that we might share it with the rest of those who love to laugh.

Summer of the Lost Ham

Canoe? Gone. Paddles? Gone. Honey-baked Georgia Ham? Gone.

By Laurie Gough

We weren't the only canoeists paddling down the Yukon River that summer. About a dozen people were paddling along the same route at the same time—from Whitehorse to the Klondike. We all had our own pace and stopped at different times, yet two or three times a day we would happen upon the same people, especially at some of the rustic campsites, which were usually abandoned miners' camps or old Indian sites. We got to know some of our fellow paddlers fairly well, all of us part of a friendly assemblage of people of varying ages and lifestyles from different countries, but all encountering the same scenery, the same rain, sunshine, and wildlife, and all with the same whimsical compulsion to paddle the Yukon River.

Even though we were in Canada, my friend Kevin and I were two of the only Canadians on the river. Most of the other canoeists were American, German, or Swiss. Every day we would pass the same spiky-haired German men—they had leather jackets, tattoos, and lots of metal bits protruding from their flesh. They were usually fishing, which seemed incongruous with their tough-guy image.

Another pair of Germans we saw only once, because they were hell-bent on making it to Dawson City as fast as possible. Since the midnight sun was up and we had twenty-four hours of daylight, they refused to waste light and were paddling around the clock.

The six women from Florida we came across at least three times a day. They were in their mid-fifties, on a college reunion, and this was their first canoe trip. Every time we came across them, they were laughing and dealing with a minor catastrophe. It always seemed that Marge was the butt of their jokes, since she insisted on applying makeup and styling her hair every day. "Mr. Right could be out here, honey, around any corner," she told me. "You just don't know!"

The Alberta Brothers was the name we gave to a pair of bald twins from Alberta, each with his own canoe equipped with a small outboard motor. The Alberta Brothers would often come ashore at a campsite for the "night" and cook dinner just as Kevin and I were finishing our breakfast and preparing to set off for the "day." The twenty-four-hour daylight was confusing. We'd wake up not knowing if it was seven a.m. or seven p.m. As time passed, I kept waiting for it to get dark. I felt as though I was missing something essential as each day passed into the next without the familiar dreamtime to replenish what the day took away. Whenever we saw them, the Alberta Brothers would never fail to ask us what time it was. We never did know the time and I never understood why it was so important to them.

"Does it really matter?" I finally asked them one morning, which was one evening for them.

They had no reply, but looked at me as if I'd told them I was holding secret meetings with the Pope deep inside the earth.

One morning as we paddled down the river we heard the high-pitched sound of a man shouting wildly. But we couldn't see him. Then we looked up to the top of a metal lookout tower beside the river, and there he was: a crazed fat man yelling at us. He was dressed in army fatigues and was nearly hysterical, waving his arms frantically. Incoherent and panic-stricken, he seemed to want desperately to tell us something. When we asked him if he wanted us to pull into shore, he shouted down, "Well, if y'all can, I'd mighty appreciate it."

We pulled in for the man, who introduced himself as Ernie. He wasn't halfway down the tower when he started telling his tale: how he and his partner, hunters from Georgia, had capsized their canoe the day before in some monstrous rapids not far ahead; how he'd swum to shore and walked hours back along the riverbank to the tower he remembered passing; and how his partner, who he thought was now probably dead, had stayed floating in the river to chase after the canoe and save the ham. Ernie didn't care about the lost case of beer. His wife was always nagging him to cut down anyway. But that mother of a honey-baked ham they had brought all the way from Georgia, they'd really been hankering after that. All that food and beer was now in the bottom of the river. It was a crying shame.

Ernie plunked himself down in the middle of our canoe, causing it to sink so deeply into the water that I feared a river disaster myself.

At that point, Ernie commenced his monologue. "Those rapids are a-comin' soon and I ain't gonna fall out again. I'm gonna hang on. My wife. I gotta call my wife. I almost died yesterday and do ya think she'll care? Probably not. I'm callin' her as soon as we get to a phone. We lost our ham, we lost our beer. Shouldn't have been sittin' up on that beer case. Too shaky. Better to sit down low like this here. Say, what part of the States are you two from?"

The Canadian part, Kevin told him.

"Hell, I gotta find my partner. I doubt he's alive."

We soon reached the "rapids" where the southern duo had met their fate—nothing more than a few barely discernable ripples on the water. How they'd managed to paddle across Lake Laberge without succumbing to the strong winds I couldn't fathom.

"It ain't what she looks like. She's a trickster, this river. Hang on."

We continued paddling, waiting for something terrible to happen. "Okay, maybe this is a better canoe. Those rapids were powerful yesterday. Nearly killed us. Jimmy, my partner, he's probably dead. Yep, won't be shootin' ducks with Jimbo no more."

Not far after the nonexistent rapids, we came across Jimbo, but Jimbo was far from dead. In fact, he was relaxing beside a campfire he'd built with his face turned into the sun. Next to him sat a sleeping pad propped on its side with the word HELP written across it in large letters.

"Howdy all," Jimmy said with a casual wave of his hand, as if this were a church picnic. "Thought you'd be showin' up soon, Ern." Jimmy, in contrast to paunchy Ernie, was long and lean.

He sported a scraggly red beard and a felt hat pulled low over his head.

We pulled ashore. Ernie hauled his massive body out of the canoe, walked up to Jimmy and grabbed hold of him. He pulled rigid Jimmy into the wide spread of his sweaty chest, displaying a degree of tenderness I found surprising from a man who'd been lamenting his beer and his honey-baked Georgia ham.

Jimmy looked vaguely bewildered. He didn't hug Ernie back, but Ernie didn't seem to notice. "We ain't dead, Jimmy, we ain't dead. I love ya, man. I love ya! Say, where the heck is our canoe?"

"Gone."

"Ham?"

"Gone"

"Where's everything else?"

"Gone."

"How'd you get this fire lit? How'd you get this here sleepin' pad?"

"Some friendly folks came by. They helped a bit. They left."

That's when it struck me for the first time: Ernie and Jimmy might ask Kevin and me to take them for the rest of the canoe trip.

I looked over at Kevin and could see the same thought was circulating through his head. A silent shudder passed between us.

But then, miraculously, we were saved. From around the bend the Alberta Brothers appeared, each with his own canoe. They even had outboard motors, which would help to lug the extra weight of Ernie.

"Come ashore," we called to them. "Have some lunch."

At first the Alberta Brothers were happy to take Ernie and Jimmy along. Apparently the twins had been fighting and were sick of each other's company. They were thankful for the distraction. But later that day, when they finally came across the Americans' upside-down canoe snagged in a mass of dead trees, the Alberta Brothers were no longer on speaking terms with Ernie. We spotted Ernie and Jimmy ahead of us on the riverbank, their damaged canoe sitting between them. Ernie jumped up and down and waved at us, while Jimmy nonchalantly lay on the ground. They were once more at the mercy of whoever came down the river. Their canoe badly needed patching and the Alberta Brothers had unceremoniously dumped them there and left.

"Stupid rednecks," said Ernie. "Tried tellin' us everything we done wrong yesterday. As if they're any smarter." Since we didn't have room for the two of them, or any patches for their canoe, we were of no use to them and free to leave.

That night at a campsite called Big Salmon, we learned that the six women from Florida had rescued Ernie and Jimmy. Marge was at the campfire with a broad smile on her face, her rouged cheeks flaming, her coiffed hair disheveled. Jimmy pulled on his beard and stole shy glances in her direction. He was a changed man, a man whose last name was apparently Right. Marge and Jimmy had fallen in love.

And so it went, the Yukon River with its never-ending light inspiring love and languor. During the day we floated and at night we reminisced, trying to relive the scenes of the river in our minds:

the eagles and the leggy moose, the impossible green of the river and the mountains rising up like sudden thoughts. The nights never failed to bring with them, on schedule and at a distinct decibel level, the not-too-distant voice of Ernie telling his story of the river disaster that almost took his life, the story of how he'd been so close to death he'd spoken to God and asked forgiveness—forgiveness for what, we never asked. The story of how he'd swum miles alone along that river, searching for his partner. It was a tale of heroic proportions that we didn't even recognize, a tale that Kevin and I, by its fifth telling, had been cut out of entirely.

"I don't understand," said a Swiss man to me one night by the campfire. "Every night we hear this same story, and every night the story grows more dangerous." The Swiss man confided that he had also passed a hysterical Ernie, but hadn't stopped for him. He simply waved at Ernie and kept paddling, thinking that the man in army fatigues must be an escaped lunatic from the military. "This happens sometimes in Switzerland," he said. "The army drives them mad and they head for the wilderness. I didn't want to go near him."

On the tenth day we looked up from the river to see a bridge in the distance. The bridge seemed intrusive and alien, and it meant that civilization was ahead. A few minutes later we passed some shacks along the water and a clearing in the forest. Sadly, we'd arrived at Carmacks and the end of our journey. Carmacks was a forgettable little town with three restaurants, all owned by the same man. This perhaps explained the ten-dollar salad we purchased, which consisted solely of iceberg lettuce.

That night, camping in our tent beside a river that almost felt like home, I thought of the drifters, homesteaders, and renegades who had tramped across an unimaginable expanse of country and boated down a river to find gold. I thought of the ones who had died along the way, their bones at the bottom of the mighty Yukon, polished and fragile. If you listen carefully you can almost hear their voices—a faint murmur in your sleep, as if the dead souls were babbling at the edge of the river. And then I thought of Ernie, whose bones the river didn't want, and whose babbling at the edge of the river was enough to waken the dead.

Lauded by Time *magazine as "one of the new generation of intrepid female travel writers," Laurie Gough is author of* Kiss the Sunset Pig: An American Road Trip with Exotic Detours *(Penguin), and* Kite Strings of the Southern Cross: A Woman's Travel Odyssey, *which was shortlisted for the Thomas Cook Travel Book Award. It was also the silver medal winner of ForeWord Magazine's Travel Book of the Year in the United States. In addition to the many newspaper and magazine articles she has had published—including features in* The Globe and Mail, The L.A. Times, Canadian Geographic, *and* The Daily Express—*twenty of Laurie's stories have been anthologized in literary travel books. You can visit her at www.lauriegough.com, as well as her blog: www.travelwritinglife.com.*

Hiking the Alps in Flip-flops

Beware of the farmer with the pitchfork.

By Ryan Clement

For trekking the Alps, most guides recommend proper footwear. A prospective hiker might select a solid cross-trainer, Gore-Tex boots with ankle support, or even crampons if they plan to cross a lot of snow and ice. I wore flip-flops.

I should explain.

Now, I'm not one of those people whose love of lightweight footwear argues against basic common sense. I was not promoting an alternative fabric-free lifestyle. I don't even like sandals. Whenever I wear them, a physics-defying rock seems to wedge itself between the sandal and my foot. I've found that covered shoes also provide protection against my tendency to stub toes on rocks, wayward logs, and anything else at ground level. A shower flip-flop is no more suitable for an alpine trek than it would be for a jaunt across the Martian tundra. I am quite aware of this.

It all began while I was in Belgium, visiting a friend during a week that happened to coincide with an impromptu family reunion. His family was very hospitable, but their Liège townhouse—despite its many floors—could only accommodate so many guests. It seemed appropriate to take a few days for a mini-adventure, so as not to hang around and make a general nuisance of myself. But where to go? I had just been to Germany, France, the Netherlands, and Luxembourg. But somehow, in all of this back-and-forth I had managed to miss Switzerland.

If you say the word Switzerland, what comes to mind? Chocolate? Cuckoo clocks? St. Bernards? Smiling, idyllic peasant girls? Neutrality? Banks with treasures stolen by Nazis? Yodeling?

You might also think of the Alps. And one way or another, the famous mountain range seems to figure into many of these other stereotypes. The chocolate you're thinking of? It's like a row of points along a base, isn't it? That St. Bernard? Probably rescued some wayward skier. Meanwhile, within view of these same mountains, peasant girls gather flowers and twirl in the fields above hidden caves filled with stolen artwork. While yodeling.

You get the picture.

Of course, being from the Canadian prairies—where hills are so exotic that we build them out of garbage—any oversized rocky outcropping was bound to leave me googly eyed until someone pointed out that there was another one just behind it. And these weren't just any mountains; these were *The Alps*, Europe's most famous mountain range. When Japan talks about its Japanese Alps or New Zealand talks about its Southern Alps, these are the mountains they are comparing their own mountains to. Not only was the word "alpine" invented here, but practically the entire sport of mountaineering was, too.

Now, I'm no Edmund Hillary, but I've skimmed a book or two by John Krakauer and walked through plenty of snow (I'm from Manitoba, after all). How hard could it be?

For many trekkers, a summit attempt requires months of preparation and an arduous journey by pack animal, rickety bus, or other rugged means just to reach the base camp. I took a train—a German one, which meant that it was clean, efficient, and reasonably comfortable. That said, there's quite a change in elevation between coastal Belgium and Switzerland. My ears popped and my head felt dizzy. Was it altitude sickness or just the carbonated water? Or the wine?

As base camps go, Zurich is hard to beat. It's a vibrant city, squeezed into a narrow valley at the drainage point of picturesque Lake Zurich. The water is clean here. People actually swim in it. As I crossed a bridge, a wave of bright yellow inner tubes—each sporting a rather relaxed Zuricher with beer stein in hand—floated underneath me like balloons in a European art film. On either side of the built-up banking district, centuries-old guild houses smiled down while snow-capped mountains beckoned to me in the distance.

It was too late in the day to do any hiking, so I rented a free bike (I love Europe) and set out to explore Switzerland's largest city. Everything was very clean, very green, and very expensive (except the free bike). The landlocked country had recently joined the borderless zone created by the Schengen Agreement, which means there are no customs officials guarding land borders, but also no euros. Instead, travelers must adapt to an entirely different and rather colorful currency: the Swiss franc, which is more than happy to help you spend more than you realize.

The Swiss are actually quite modern, despite what the aforementioned stereotypes might lead some to believe. Indeed, they would probably prefer that visitors leave these stereotypes at home—or at least not bring them up in conversation. Nevertheless, I saw plenty of fondue and even a cheese-rolling competition in the Zurich train station, so in my opinion they have only themselves to blame. Besides, when you have a country as beautiful as this one, who wouldn't invent ridiculously complicated pocketknives to defend it?

Tired from all the cycling, I headed back to the hostel. After all, I needed to save some energy for the next day. The Alps weren't going to climb themselves.

On the way, I stopped to buy my train ticket to adventure, which is when I discovered a route into neighboring Liechtenstein, a tiny geographic anomaly of a country sandwiched between Austria and Switzerland. According to my guidebook, Liechtenstein is a traveler's delight of eccentricity. The world's largest exporter of false teeth? Check. A country that abolished its army after they failed to arrive at their last war on time? Check. A principality ruled by a strong monarch who lives in a gothic castle on a hill and has the entire population over for beer once a year? Check and double-check.

Plus, Liechtenstein is actually said to be the place where the Eastern and Western Alps meet. An arbitrary distinction, I'm sure, but as good an excuse as any to pay a visit. So I bought a nonrefundable ticket, returned to my hostel, rode the tiny dumbwaiter-cum-elevator to an upper floor, and plopped myself into bed for the night.

The next morning I got up at the crack of ten and began preparing. While there was no bathroom in my room (this being a hostel), there was a sink, which made it a far cry better than most hostels. Not wanting to pass up this luxury of luxuries, I used the communal shower and then returned to my room to shave.

Being both a backpacker and a typical man, I had only two pairs of shoes with me: my well-worn and undoubtedly pungent runners and a pair of six-dollar flip-flops. The flip-flops were purchased for the sole purpose of preventing my feet from touching the communal shower floor. Why I was wearing my sneakers is a mystery lost to the masses.

I had noticed the crack in the sink the night before. Such nicks and scratches are common in sinks all over the world, and most sinks still mange to maintain structural integrity. Nevertheless, this crack was like a palm reader's lifeline and a portent of doom.

As men go, some might say I'm a sizable gent. Standing at over six feet tall and well over two hundred pounds, lightweight is not an adjective that I hear used very often to describe me (except perhaps sarcastically).

Pop quiz: what happens when a sizable gent like *moi* hunches down and leans on the sink to aid in shaving? No sense in getting nicked by the razor, after all.

Answer: the sink this sizable gent is leaning on unceremoniously snaps in two.

Naturally, I was wearing nothing but a white hostel towel, which provided no protection from the porcelain daggers that were flung from the sink during its death throes. The sink cleaved deep gouges on my right hand and upper leg, before shattering completely on the ground.

Initially, I was too befuddled to feel pain. I just stared dumbfounded at the fountain of water and the geyser of blood pooling on the floor. Eventually, it occurred to me that I might need medical attention.

I shambled out of the room, still wearing nothing but my sneakers and my towel, one hand applying pressure to my leg and the other applying pressure to itself and trying to keep the towel up.

I called the elevator.

The numbers slowly flickered on and off. I could see it approaching my floor, and when the door opened, several passengers were already inside.

We stared at each other. It was apparent that they had not expected to find a large, half-naked man standing in front of them, wanting to board the elevator.

I lurched forward anyway and squeezed between them, manually closing the latch door behind me. The elevator began descending. Gentle elevator music played.

On the ground floor, I shuffled past the breakfast room, the TV room, and the pub to the front desk, my bloody wake marking my trail like a scene from a macabre Hansel and Gretel.

The front desk girl was speechless. I opened the conversation.

"Uh … guten morgen?" Zurich is in the predominantly German-speaking part of Switzerland, but they don't like calling it German here or even being compared to Germany. In fact, forget I made that Hansel and Gretel reference.

"Uh … sprechen sie Englisch?"

The girl still stared at me.

"Nein."

Things were not going well, but becoming proficient in the local language—while advisable when traveling abroad—is an activity best left for moments when one has a self-contained blood supply. Or is at least fully clothed.

Eventually, through an elaborate means of impromptu charades, unintentional exhibitionism, and the international distress signal of a spurting blood vessel, I managed to communicate my request for first aid and possibly a change of room. She called her manager.

To their credit, once the opportunity to perform first aid presented itself, the Swiss attacked it with vigor. They are, after all, the founders of the Red Cross. Soon I was sanitized, anaesthetized, and cauterized in places I didn't even know were bleeding. To restore my fluids—and perhaps to reduce the odds of a lawsuit—they gave me drink after drink, also wrapping enough bandages around me to make me vaguely resemble a central European mummy.

Naturally they wanted to take my towel, which though bloodied and in need of cleaning, was the only thing preserving what dignity I had left. My sneakers, previously a grubby white-black, had by this time taken on a decidedly reddish hue.

With my wounds addressed, my main concern became the acquisition of pants—but returning to my room, now a quarantined crime scene, was impossible. They offered me an alternative room and helped me get my bags (and pants), after which I began to feel slightly more respectable again.

At this point, a wiser man would have given up on his original plan.

But I had come this far. I had bled, I had bruised, and I had spent my Swiss francs. Something like this wouldn't have stopped Edmund Hillary or Tenzing Norgay (or even Richard Branson), and it sure as hell wasn't gonna stop me!

Of course, there was now a slight problem. After confiscating my bloodied towel for cleaning purposes, the friendly hostel staff also helped themselves to my shoes. They told me I would get them back when the blood had been washed out. I suppose I should have been grateful that they were being cleaned for me (they probably hadn't seen soap since the day I purchased them), but they were the only pair of legitimate shoes I had. I needed them for walking and such.

My desperate pleas fell on deaf ears as my clodhoppers tumbled and tumbled in the washing machine. As my train's scheduled departure neared, I found myself forced to make a critical decision: miss the train and spend the day at the hostel nursing my wounds, or follow the spirit of adventure/stupidity and tackle the Alps in flip-flops?

I think by now you know which path I took.

Arriving at the Swiss-Liechtenstein border, a brightly colored bus picked up the would-be Liechtenstein visitors—all five of us—and headed to the capital of Vaduz.

As European capitals go, Vaduz isn't exactly Paris. Considering that the entire country has a population of just over thirty thousand, the vibe is decidedly rural, even compared to Luxembourg. Having said that, there are still enough art galleries, cafés, and museums dedicated to obscure Central European history to allow visitors to while away an afternoon.

But the highlight is the mountain overlooking the town, which houses the imposing Vaduz Castle, the prince's estate.

This was my mountain.

I meandered my way up the well-groomed but steep pathway, keeping my flip-flops delicately balanced beneath my feet. I concentrated hard to avoid those wayward physics-defying pebbles that always get stuck in one's sandals.

I reached the castle. A sign said: NOT OPEN TO THE PUBLIC.

So much for the free beer. No matter; I would push on to the summit.

I hiked through a mixed forest of deciduous and coniferous trees, passed creeks, and climbed several steep staircases. I stopped to examine a crazy green fungus that might have blown in from Chernobyl. I stumbled a lot, yes, but I was already bandaged, so I didn't come to further harm.

Eventually I reached a high-altitude meadow and what was, for me, a living, breathing Alpine utopia.

The meadow was decidedly steep—back home we would have called it a cliff. On its higher reaches, among the grazing goats, a traditionally attired peasant girl scythed wheat. On closer inspection, she was probably in her eighties, but seemed in better shape than I'd ever be.

At first, I thought this stereotypical mountain scene must have been staged by the Liechtenstein Tourism Board. But then I spotted an equally old man—ostensibly her husband—pushing his wheelbarrow toward me. He was attired in suspenders and shorts that I would be tempted to call lederhosen, were I not concerned about comparing him to a German (or if he was a German, comparing him to a Bavarian).

At any rate, I needn't have worried, because the man clearly couldn't speak a lick of English and, in fact, was as surprised to see me as if I had stepped out of a time machine. He picked up a pitchfork and gave me the kind of look that farmers back home would call the what-the-hell-are-you-doing-on-my-property look.

While I had not yet reached the top of the mountain, I decided that I had endured enough blisters and near-disasters for one day. Idyllic though the meadow was, it was time to leave the wanton trespassing of private property to future travelers. I flip-flopped my way back to Vaduz and then on to Zurich, where I was ceremoniously reunited with my squeaky clean and lemon-scented sneakers.

The next day I swam in the lake. It was uneventful.

Overall, while the hardships I endured can't be compared to those of great adventurers like Hillary or Tenzing, I still finished with a tale to tell and the scars to prove it.

From my perch at the farm, apart from the sweeping views of mountains, I had witnessed the mighty Rhine River carving out its banks and an entire country laid at my feet. It was simply magical—pitchfork guy or not—and well worth the effort to get there.

Next time, though, I'll pack extra shoes.

Originally from Brandon, Manitoba, Ryan Clement has meandered his way across five continents and through sixty countries, living and working in exotic places like Johannesburg, Taipei, and Winnipeg. He also spent two years in Toronto, where he wrote a graphic novel for his master's thesis in Communication and Culture and pulled off a show at the Second City Training Centre and Toronto Fringe Festival. In addition to writing fiction, non-fiction, scripts, comics, board games, and even letters to his Mom occasionally, Ryan has been trying to crack into the elusive travel writing industry. For more information about his work—as well as his many adventures and misadventures—visit him online at www.clomy.ca.

Moose on the Loose

An epic journey with a moose named Amos.

By Sylvia Shawcross

I never did tell my sister that I was the one who invited Amos on our trip. She'd never have forgiven me if she knew. I was ten and she was fifteen, and there are some things fifteen-year-olds simply can't forgive their younger siblings.

The event I'm referring to happened back in 1970. Our family was moving from New Brunswick to Saskatchewan, and on our front lawn in Fredericton sat a gigantic moving truck that had been filled to within an inch of its carrying capacity. There was not room for a single item more. The movers—weary and shell-shocked by the sheer magnitude of what they had just accomplished—were about to close the door and leave. My family was all there except for my sister Anne, who we planned to pick up along the way at a campground in Deep River, Ontario. My mother was standing on the front porch, her arm draped around Amos. She was looking at my father expectantly.

"There's just no room," my father said.

At this I started to cry. I like to think now that it was because I had a sensitive nature, but more likely it was because I was a peculiar child who would grow up to be a writer. Nevertheless, at the time I just couldn't bear the thought of our worldly belongings being taken away by strangers to a place I didn't even want to go. The thought of leaving Amos behind pretty much ended the brave face I'd reluctantly adopted. My brother Charles, a thirteen-year-old, called me a crybaby. But I swear his lower lip was trembling just a little.

How could we possibly leave Amos?

So my father did what any loving father would do: he went over to the truck and he poked and prodded and pushed. But it was no use. There was simply no room for Amos.

"We could donate it to somebody," my father suggested, which made me cry even more.

"It's just a stupid moose head," my brother decreed.

But Amos wasn't just a moose head. Amos surely must have been the largest (not to mention finest) moose head on this side of the Rockies, at least in the humble opinion of his owners. My parents had bought him from an antique dealer where he had been languishing on a dusty floor. He had a rack of antlers with no less than a dozen and a half points, and a massive hooked snout that surrounded his hairy smile. At home, I sometimes felt his gaze following me around, keeping me company, and for that reason it was easy to strike up a conversation with Amos. The others talked to Amos, too. He was part of the family.

It was my job at Christmas to decorate Amos, hanging tree ornaments from each of his points. The rest of the year we placed fishing rods, pool cues, and easels across his fine antlers. For Halloween we made him wear a witch's hat, and sometimes in the summer we would hang sticky flypaper on his antlers because he was near the screen door. He even provided refuge to a mad cat that we had temporarily taken in; the cat hated people and spent most of her days lolling on Amos's head, hissing and growling and occasionally pouncing on unsuspecting victims who passed below. I think she thought Amos was her mother.

Considering all of this, was there any way we could leave without Amos? I think not.

"Now, Roy," said my mother, using that bewitching tone of hers that pretty much made my father do whatever she wanted.

My father sighed heavily and wandered off to look at our Volkswagen van, which was also packed to capacity.

My father and brother, taking great pride in their work, had packed the van with military precision. They had rolled what needed to be rolled, flattened what needed to be flattened, and filled in all the empty space by squishing anything that could be squished into the final remaining cavities. The back end of the van housed the birdcage with the three mynah birds that whooped and whistled and muttered. The back seat was packed to allow just enough room for my brother on one side, my sister on the other, and a cage with Lavinia and Rebecca—our two huge tomcats—in between. They were hostile with the indignity of it all. The middle half-seat was mine, which I would share occasionally with Rajah the dog, a large hairy half-breed who was supposed to stay on the floor, but who deeply resented the whole idea. The suitcases were carefully stowed beneath the back seats, and a box of books was shoved under mine. Between the two front seats was the cooler full of sandwiches and drinks. And at my mother's feet was the medicine bag: a purse full of cures for whatever ailment her family might come down with on our trip across the country. Quite clearly, there was no room for a giant moose head anywhere in this cramped space.

More suitcases and boxes were tied down under a tarp on the roof, which in the end was the only place my father could have realistically tied Amos. With great annoyance he rearranged the roof, placing Amos at the very front. The moose's nose was carefully wrapped in a plastic polka-dot tablecloth, and his head swathed tightly in a gray tarp with his bare antlers poking out the sides. Taking up a third of the roof, Amos certainly did present quite the picture. My mother and I both smiled, and I suspect my brother did too. Not that he would have admitted it or anything. Amos was on the roof and all was right with the world again.

In the morning we set off on our journey.

There are two inevitabilities of any family road trip: siblings left together in the back of a car will start fighting, and ipso facto, parents need to stop for tea or coffee on a regular basis. My father's beverage of choice was two-bag tea steeped in almost-boiling water.

There was also a third inevitable variable we had to deal with: disgruntled animals. The cats howled and paced restlessly in their cage, while the mynah birds—perhaps in response to the passing scenery—wolf-whistled and cackled loudly. The dog stared belligerently at me from the floor for the first hour, until he eventually moved up to sit half across my lap, which is where he would stay for the most of the trip. Then he got carsick, and we were forced to pull over before he vomited all over everything. We fed him anti-nausea pills for the rest of the trip.

My brother, a wannabe musician, began drumming the back of my seat with a pair of spoons. He "played" *Sweet City Woman* over and over and over again, which wouldn't have been so bad except he also fancied himself a singer. And as anyone will tell you after listening to my brother, he is no singer. He emits a sound that is more like a low-pitched growl. The dog did not take it well. Eventually the dog began howling along.

And then there was Amos, and the effect he seemed to have on people.

Cars honked from behind us. People waved as they sped past in the opposing lane. It felt like we were the grand masters of a parade heading north: a bright red box on wheels with a polka-dot moose head at the front end of the float. We made it to Woodstock, New Brunswick before my parents, already disheveled and exasperated, made our first pit stop. And so began a routine that was repeated at every pit stop along the way.

We always tried to park the van close to the window of the restaurants we ate at so that we could see it clearly. The back flap was usually left open to air out the interior for the sake of the birds, which inevitably drew a crowd. My mother would give the dog some anti-nausea pills, and my brother would take him for a walk. It was my job to walk the cats.

Walking the cats turned out to be rather humiliating. They would climb trees or squirm under bushes where they would dig in their claws and meow angrily. They were hell-bent on escape for the entire trip and eventually I started complaining that I shouldn't be the one who always had to walk them. I never did win the argument. My brother liked to remind me at every opportunity that they were "my" cats and therefore "my" responsibility. He was no doubt feeling annoyed that he had to rescue the irate, tangled furballs whenever they climbed a tree.

My father's primary duty was to get us across the country in one piece, and therefore he felt it was also his duty to relax a little bit whenever we stopped—to have a piece of freshly baked pie and a hot cup of tea. But perhaps most importantly, he accepted the responsibility of explaining Amos to inquiring strangers.

You have to understand one thing about my father: he was not a hunter. At one time we had a lot of chickens running free-range over our New Brunswick property, but this was because my father—despite his best intentions—could never bring himself to actually kill one. We owned a gun, but it sat empty on Amos's antlers and was mainly just for show. Nevertheless, due to boredom or because my father had a mischievous side, he suddenly became a big-game hunter on this journey. Smiling and swaggering, he would regale his audience with a story about how he had shot Amos on a hunting trip in Newfoundland. The audience lapped it up.

"Since when did you start hunting big game?" my mother asked after the first episode.

"Oh, they just wanted a story," he said, smiling. "I just thought I would oblige."

By the time we reached Edmundston, New Brunswick, the town knew we were coming. We were the talk of the road up and down the line. The waitress happily made a hot cup of tea for my father and insisted on giving him an extra slice of apple pie so that he could finish his moose story. My mother swallowed her tea the wrong way and had a coughing fit.

When we were back in the car my mother had words with him. "Where on earth did you ever learn to parachute?"

"Oh, just a little exaggeration," my father said. He was grinning broadly.

"So let me get this straight," she said. "You were parachuting with a loaded gun over Churchill Falls, and you just happened to shoot a moose on the way down?"

"I got two pieces of pie for that one," he said triumphantly.

The next province was Quebec, and in retrospect we were lucky to get out of there in one piece. Mostly this was because my father liked to pretend he could speak French, cleverly (in his mind) reciting one-liners such as: "Common si diddly-poop and the bow-wow sitting on the back door step woof-woof." In retrospect, it was not the best idea on the eve of the FLQ crisis. There was also a group of Hell's Angels that decided to escort us from Quebec City to Montreal, whooping and hollering all the way. They had obviously taken a shine to Amos.

We stopped at a dingy little diner somewhere in la belle province where, much to his relief, my father found a willing audience for his new moose story in English. My father had a fine piece of sugar pie and only one cat climbed a tree.

"You realize, Roy," my mother said, "that it is quite possible they were only humoring you. Nobody in their right mind would believe you lassoed a moose from a canoe in Happy Valley and had it pull you all the way down the river to Rigolet before it died of exhaustion."

"It could have happened," he said. "Stranger things have happened. And who, I might add, insisted we bring Amos in the first place?"

All I remember about Parliament Hill was our dog's attempted escape and the uniformed security guard. As we pulled up to the front and piled out of the car, Rajah decided to make a run for it. The mynahs started wolf-whistling as my brother chased the dog around the impeccably manicured front lawn. The security guard watched my brother run around in circles for the longest time before he politely suggested that we leave. The dog, seeing that we were about to depart without him, crashed into the guard and knocked him over on his way back to the van. Apparently the guard wasn't interested in my father's moose story. This had a profound effect on my father, because he'd been working on it since Montreal. This meant we would have to stop somewhere before Deep River for more tea and pie.

"Now, Roy," my mother said, "Have you considered what you are teaching *your* children with all these tall tales? Have you ever considered what people must think when you tell them we hit a moose in New Brunswick, and we're now roasting the meat at the side of the road every night on our way to Saskatchewan? There isn't even a dent on the van, for heaven's sake!"

"Nobody's noticed so far," my father said.

My brother and I had settled down with some books—I had Farley Mowat's *The Boat Who Wouldn't Float*, and he had a copy of some World War II nonsense about Green Berets. We had started reading because we knew a heated discussion between our parents was about to begin. We knew this because Mother had referred to us as "your children." The dog howled during the entire argument, which my father may have lost in principle, but which apparently did not deter him one bit. The stories continued.

Although it doesn't seem possible, I recall that we could see the look on my sister's face from the far end of that long driveway in Deep River. As we approached with our polka-dot moose head, howling dog, and whistling mynahs, her eyes grew wider, her face grew redder, and she seemed to back away. At her side, the new boyfriend was trying to say something. By the time we pulled up in front of the campground, people had already come out to see what was going on. When we opened the door, my sister had vanished.

It took two hours to convince her that she had to come with us, even if she preferred at that point to be an orphan for the rest of her life. She insisted that we had to wait for dark before she would climb into the van, and even then she tried to disguise herself with a very large hat and scarf. This was fine for my father because he had a few good stories to relate, the telling of which only made my sister angrier. She cowered in the back seat for the rest of the trip, cursing the mynah birds for whistling and threatening to personally strangle my brother if he didn't stop singing. I was glad to finally have an ally on that subject. So was the dog.

In Winnipeg, the engine on the old van died and we spent a week having it repaired. This suited my mother fine; I guess she figured that if we used the same diner, my father's deeply tragic tale of nearly freezing to death while moose hunting in Alaska with a bow and arrow would only be told once. Still, I seem to recall that it was enough to get him a complimentary slice of blackberry pie every day for the whole week. I also discovered that walking cats in a thunderstorm is a deeply traumatic experience.

By the time we reached Saskatchewan, my mother was apoplectic with exasperation.

"Roy, you're just being absurd now! Four-year-old boys trying to protect their mothers from a marauding moose do not kill a fifteen-hundred-pound animal with a pocketknife! How can you even tell such a story with a straight face?"

"Saskatoon berry pie," said my father happily.

When we arrived at our new home in Meadow Lake, the first thing we took into the house was Amos. He almost looked a little drab after being wrapped in the polka dots for so long. But no matter; Amos had made it to Saskatchewan with the rest of his family, and the fact that he would once again be watching over us made it feel just like home.

The funniest thing was how this trip changed my father. For years afterward, I'd catch him polishing Amos's glass eyes with a handkerchief. When I'd ask him why, he would just smile and tell me that he was reliving his glory days, such as they were.

Sylvia Shawcross lives in the forested hills of Chelsea, Quebec, but her heart belongs to the Maritimes. She writes a humour column for The West Quebec Post, *and is the author of two books:* Never Mind All That *and* The Get-Over-Yourself Self-Help Book. *In the words of Farley Mowat, she is "that rarity of our times, an honest-to-god satirist." As such, Shawcross loves to rail against the insanity of our world in her unique curmudgeonly style.*

One Little Ounce

Sometimes that's all you need.

By Barbara McAlear

Here's a little lesson proving once and for all that an ounce of prevention is definitely better than a pound of cure.

For many years our family owned a small cottage on an island located in Georgian Bay, Ontario, surrounded by beautiful white sand beaches and wonderfully clean water. Our neighbors, Frank and Diane, had a family of seven children and a shaggy mutt dog.

Island children, no matter whom they belonged to, were treated as extended family by most of the cottagers. We formed something of a loose-knit family: everybody was included in water-skiing events, corn roasts, card games, singing and dancing around bonfires in the sand, or playing silly word or number games while sitting around the campfire.

There was no television at the cottage, so adults and children learned to read and enjoy books. We happily learned about each other and watched our families grow up.

Because we were on an island, everybody had to pull together. If one cottager needed a plunger or a widget, they would inevitably find one at somebody else's cottage.

As it happened, Frank and my husband Al were sitting on Frank's deck one weekend chatting about his family's cranky septic system, which is a topic of long and thought-provoking conversation among cottagers everywhere. Due to the fact that Frank had such a large family, they had friends visiting nearly every weekend; as a result, his septic system was beginning to show a little wear and tear. My husband, being familiar with wells and water pumping systems, suggested that Frank should put a bit of yeast in the septic tank to activate it, which he assured Frank would get it going again.

Frank had never heard of such a thing, but readily agreed to give it a try. He and my husband took Frank's boat and sped off to the mainland village to pick up some yeast.

That evening, Frank waited until most of his family had gone to bed for the night before adding the yeast. Although my husband had suggested putting in only a few ounces, Frank figured that more was better, and therefore dropped in the entire package. He was going to make sure that he unplugged his septic system on the first attempt.

All was quiet and serene that next morning. At around ten o'clock, my husband and I decided to go for a walk along the beach. As usual, we met other cottagers on our walk and sat down in the sand to have a gossip, to watch the boats pass by, and possibly to cadge a cup of coffee while enjoying the beautiful sunny day.

It was at some point during this conversation that we heard an unusual rumbling sound building to our right. Everyone turned to see what was going on. Suddenly, from the point where Frank's cottage jutted slightly into the bay, we heard a massive explosion. The next thing we knew, a geyser had erupted from the back of his property, which began raining toilet paper and other "fragments" down over the roof of Frank's cottage and the nearby trees.

His septic tank was erupting!

At almost the exact same moment, every door in the cottage opened and began to spew out adults, children, and dogs, in various states of undress. All were craning their necks toward the sky to see what was going on. You might guess that some of the remarks coming from the cottage's inhabitants were unusually colorful.

Everyone else could hardly stand up, we were laughing so hard.

After the hubbub was over, Frank and family spent the rest of the day cleaning up the aftermath of his "pound of cure." But to this day, his family continues to suffer good-natured ribbing from their many island neighbors.

Barbara McAlear's family no longer owns the cottage on Christian Island, but they remember fondly the many family gatherings at their "home away from home." This is her second story for a Summit Studios anthology. She is also the author of Blue Window Van, which appeared in Never Trust a Smiling Bear.

Monkey Business

When a small, furry companion becomes a dictator.

By Rita Pomade

We were an assorted crew sailing out on the China Sea, sprawled on the deck of the *Santa Rita*, chugging down Tsingtao beer and gorging on shrimp chips. The *Santa Rita* was a 45-foot ketch that my husband Bernard and I had built in Taiwan. The crew was made up of some of the colleagues with whom I taught English at the British Council. I had invited them for a day of rest and relaxation aboard our boat.

It was a miserably hot day. A slight breeze offered some relief, but not enough to wake us from our lethargy. Bernard decided to rig a makeshift chair under the boom, which he extended out from the yacht. We took turns sitting on the chair with the wind at our backs and skimming the waves with our toes. It was the only relief we had from the heat.

Most of us were settled into a comfortable stupor, waiting our turn, when Bernard called out that he'd spotted an octopus about ten yards off the stern on the leeward side. Skepticism and the weight of our perspiration kept us glued to our seats. We were far more interested in not missing out on the chair-ride than in whatever flotsam was bobbing around in the sea.

Bernard, an independent soul, took no notice of our lethargy. Despite our protests, he lowered the sails to slow the yacht's speed, jumped into the dinghy, primed its engine, and set off for a closer look at his discovery. He was back in less than five minutes with a repulsive-looking thing slung over the crook of his arm.

My first impression was that the object was a large rat—a waterlogged creature one step from death. Its limp, gray form hung motionless over Bernard's arm like a dishrag. A thick cord was knotted around its neck, a soggy piece of which trailed along the deck.

Ahmad, a Malay fisherman Bernard had invited along, was the first to speak. "It's a monkey," he said. "Maybe drowned."

He walked over to Bernard, took the limp creature from his arm, and laid it on the deck seat. He breathed into its mouth and pumped the little arms. The matted ball of fur gurgled and spit up some water, like a tiny fountain. It opened its eyes and stared at us while we cheered its miraculous resurrection.

Ahmad looked up. "It's a baby, a female," he said. "Maybe six months old."

We moved away to give it some space, but we couldn't take our eyes off the tiny form. "I didn't know monkeys could swim," I said.

"She's a crab-eating macaque," Ahmed said. "They swim." He took a penknife from his pocket and cut through the cord tied around her neck. "She's probably contraband. Monkeys aren't allowed in Singapore without papers. But rich people pay a lot to eat their brains. It's not legal, but people still want them. They're smuggled in from Indonesia. The smugglers must have seen a customs boat and threw her overboard." He turned to Bernard. "She's been swimming a long time. Probably wouldn't have made it if you hadn't seen her."

The monkey appeared to be listening to every word the fisherman said. She didn't take her eyes off of him, and as he talked, she was growing noticeably stronger. To our surprise, she jumped off the seat and onto the deck—still fragile, but determined. She moved from person to person, chattering nonstop. "I think she's desperate to tell us her story," I said. "Or perhaps she's thanking us." It was hard to know what was going on in that little head.

It was love at first sight for Bernard. He scooped up the tiny body with one of his huge hands and sat her on his palm. "I'm going to name her Lola," he told us. He looked the monkey straight in the eyes, and said, "Welcome aboard, mate."

The savior and agitated ball of fur stared each other down. Neither one blinked. Eventually, Bernard broke into an idiotic grin.

The first night Lola wouldn't stop crying, so we wrapped her in a small blanket and brought her into our berth. She insisted on sleeping between us and fussed if she was pushed to the edge. The first morning of our *ménage a trois*, we discovered that toilet training was going to be an issue. We couldn't walk her like a dog, and she didn't have the fastidious nature of a cat. Our berth was a stinky mess.

We discussed what to do about her dreadful toilet habits. I told Bernard that she was his monkey, and that he'd have to find a solution. He went ashore in search of a box of Pampers.

On his return, he took out a pair and carefully cut a hole for her tail. The Pampers were sized for infants and came up to her armpits, but she was willing to keep them on. I made it clear that changing her was his responsibility.

Lola grew more beautiful each day. Her dull coat began to shine under Bernard's diligent grooming. Then one day she began to groom herself. From that moment on, gratitude was dead. She quickly forgot that she owed us anything. Her appealing, almost modest nature morphed into that of a little tyrant. Lola emerged from her piteous shell to become a spoiled and unmanageable child, given to sneaky thefts and pouting when reprimanded. Worse, Bernard became head honcho, while I was relegated to lowest person on our totem of three. Every time Bernard disciplined Lola, she slapped me hard on the leg.

Lola spent hours grooming Bernard. She inspected every hair on his legs and arms. From time to time she stopped, looked at her fingers, and slipped a speck of something into her mouth. For the life of me, I couldn't see anything and couldn't imagine what she was harvesting.

In turn, he spent hours grooming her, pretending to pick specks off of her coat and putting them into his mouth. It was a ritual that she enjoyed, and it kept her out of trouble for a short time.

On her more expansive days, Lola even groomed me, her nimble fingers inspecting every inch of my scalp. And as she did with Bernard, she would stop from time to time to take some questionable thing off of my head to eat.

After she had groomed me, she would sit on my shoulder and stare at my hand as I wrote. Writing both fascinated and perplexed her. It was always when I was hunched over the little table in the aft cabin, writing in my journal, that she would decide that I was most in need of a "makeover." She never tired of watching me move my hand across the page. Somehow this endeared her to me, and I would momentarily forget what a naughty girl she could be.

Lola followed Bernard everywhere and became agitated if he was out of her sight for any length of time. She could distinguish the sound of our dingy from all the others in the harbor, and whenever she heard him returning from shore, she would dance with excitement and dash up the galley stairs to greet him.

She imitated everything that Bernard did. He rolled his own cigarettes. Lola wanted to roll her own too. She was actually pretty good at it, although I was constantly picking up bits of tobacco and paper. At first I thought it was funny. Then she started handling the matches and the scene lost its humor. Tobacco, paper, and matches were securely locked away. But that wasn't easy, since Lola could open just about anything and inspected the contents of the lockers daily.

Aside from feeding her, everything relating to Lola was Bernard's responsibility. She saw me as an intruder on their boat. I was tolerated, but not indulged. Basically, I was relegated to the dual role of housekeeper and cook.

Unfortunately, all acts of food preparation enthralled her, and I learned that I couldn't turn my back on her for a second. To keep her out of trouble, I fed her peanuts while I cooked. She stuffed them into her cheeks until she looked liked a chipmunk, and then begged for more. When I ran out, she would hide in a corner and take them out of her mouth to be eaten one by one, hidden from my view lest I discover her subterfuge and take the extra peanuts away—or worse, ask her to share.

My status improved when my father-in-law came for a brief visit. There was now a lower person in the hierarchy. So low, in fact, that he was subject to bites after a Lola-Bernard argument. The poor man spent his entire vacation gripping a flashlight to ward off her attacks. When he saw Lola coming, he would bop her on the head. She eventually got the message and kept her distance, but it was an uneasy truce.

During a day's sail to Malaysia, Lola and Bernard had words. The sails were up and a light breeze was pushing the ketch at a nice speed. Lola was having a fine time jumping from mast to mast, something she liked to do when the boat was moving with the sails unfurled. But for some reason she couldn't let go of that last argument they'd had. At one point, she swooped down and grabbed the flashlight from my unsuspecting father-in-law and threw it overboard. Bernard was angry. He went after her, but Lola was too quick. The two yelled at each other as Bernard chased her around the deck. Eventually, just as he was about to grab her, she jumped overboard.

I figured that was it. Lola was gone. I knew she would never make it back onto a moving boat. My heartfelt sadness, tinged with relief, was replaced by disbelief when I saw her tiny head poke up over the stern—soaking wet and triumphant.

We later discussed what we should do with this unpredictable creature. It was a delicate subject. Bernard loved her, but the situation was getting serious. She was getting into everything on the boat, so we couldn't leave her behind when we went to shore. And because she had no papers, we always had to hide her in a shoulder bag when we took her with us. She couldn't be trusted around matches. She had already eaten the teak off one of the lockers under the sink in the galley, and was starting on another.

I suggested taking her to the zoo, but Bernard couldn't do it. We were at a stalemate. It was a big problem with no obvious solution.

Several days later, we were invited to a party at the home of one of my colleagues. We couldn't leave Lola behind. We'd already tried putting her in a bucket suspended from the ceiling, with a net fastened overtop, before going out. While we were gone, she had managed to swing the bucket from side to side and, with a hand stretched through the net, had shredded the curtains covering the portholes in the salon.

So we shoved her into a shoulder bag and took her with us. Our idea was to tie her to a bedpost in the bedroom of our host. However, within minutes of her confinement, she had ripped apart the bedding. Our host was not amused. Lola had gone from a novelty to a liability.

"She has to go," I said.

This time Bernard agreed with me.

The next day, we took her to the Singapore zoo. The zookeeper told us that they generally don't take domesticated monkeys because they can't adjust, but Lola was still young and he thought she might get adopted into the group. We went with her to the monkey house and saw that there were about a dozen monkeys that looked exactly like her.

We felt the adjustment would be easy. But Lola saw it differently. She looked at the fellow members of her species and was terrified. She had no idea what they were. The zookeeper assured us that she would be OK. We told him that we would come back in a few days to see how she was doing.

When we returned a week later, Lola was part of the pack. It was even hard to differentiate her from the others, and she had lost all interest in us.

The last day we saw Lola was hard on Bernard. He'd saved her life, and she had a special place in his heart. As for Lola, although gratitude wasn't high on her list of priorities, it was clear that she had felt something for Bernard. But she was a crab-eating macaque, and as a fish-eating monkey, she had other fish to fry. So did we, and we set sail for Thailand a short while later.

Rita Pomade spent seven years with her husband on a sailing adventure that took them from the China Sea to the Mediterranean. During those years they encountered pirates, scamps, madmen and dreamers. Dropping anchor wherever they pleased and for as long as they wanted, they often found more adventure than they bargained for. This story was adapted from a book that Rita is now writing about their travels.

Dinner with Nine Men

They looked like nice guys.

By Angela Goodman

While driving around Malaysia's beautiful countryside, I came across a delightful seaside town named Kuantan, located halfway up the east coast. I checked into a hotel with a view of the South China Sea, and while doing so, noticed a menu that advertised a meal called Steamboat. The name intrigued me, so I went to investigate.

By the time I arrived at the restaurant, it was early evening and twilight had set in. I noticed that the tables and chairs were all made of dark rattan and that huge palm trees stood in every corner, surrounded by colorful and exotic hanging plants. The dining area was on a partially open rooftop that was fanned by warm sea breezes, with endless views of the ocean. Tropical plants and vegetation enveloped the brightly lit swimming pool below.

The restaurant was empty except for nine Malaysian men, who were seated at a large round table covered by a blue-white batik tablecloth. At the center of the table I could see an enormous bowl that contained a steaming concoction of rice, seafood, Chinese vegetables, and various other ingredients. The aroma of herbal spices and a delicious mélange of garlic and ginger permeated the air. The meal itself reminded me of a dog's dinner, but of course with a lot more appeal.

"That looks interesting," I remarked. "Is that the Steamboat?"

"Yes," said one of the men. "Would you like to join us?"

"Oh, no, I couldn't possibly," I replied, although secretly I hoped they would insist.

The same man motioned to the waiter to bring another chair, then asked me to sit down.

The head of the group was a heavyset man with horn-rimmed glasses named Tan, who appeared to be around forty. Tan explained that he was the president of the Hong Kong Bank and that the party was in his honor, celebrating his promotion and transfer to Kuala Lumpur.

The men were very attentive, possibly because I was a blonde female Caucasian. I immediately became the centre of attention. They asked where I was from and I told them Vancouver, Canada.

"What are you doing alone in Malaysia?" Tan asked.

"I'm on vacation," I replied. I explained that I had rented a car, and that I planned to see as much of their country as possible in three weeks. "From what I've seen," I continued. "Malaysia is truly beautiful and the people are very charming."

"Where are you going next?" asked another man named Mustafa. He exhaled a thick puff of cigar smoke in my direction. Through the haze, I could see the outline of a happy face with a dark moustache and hair to match. He said that he was the vice president of the bank.

"I'll probably drive up the coast, then head west to Penang and down to Kuala Lumpur. I haven't made any reservations, so I'm free to do as I please."

"Aren't you afraid of driving alone in a strange country?" asked a third man, an older gentleman with gray hair.

"Oh no, I *love* traveling alone. It gives me the freedom to see and do whatever I want. Besides, I invariably meet lots of interesting people—like tonight, for instance."

The men chuckled.

Between puffs on his cigarette, a plump man with a salt-and-pepper beard seated to my left said, "If you're driving across the country, don't drive at night. It's a quiet, lonely road and could prove to be dangerous. I don't advise you to cross the country without stopping either. Spend the night in the mountains at a place called Gadang. It's about two-thirds of the way to Penang. It's beautiful and peaceful there." All the men agreed.

The travel recommendations continued at a mile a minute.

A distinguished middle-aged man who was sitting directly across from me said, "If you like old architecture, you'll love Georgetown. And try to see Taiping also. It's a bit inland, but it has a breathtaking park surrounded by mountains on a lovely lake. And if you are interested in caves, there are some extraordinary Hindu caves called Batu just outside Kuala Lumpur. They're a hundred and twenty million years old and reveal a major site of preserved nature." He went on to describe the large, colorful religious sculptures that were inside, and to warn me about the monkeys that I would probably see. "They bite," he said. "So be careful."

"Do you enjoy sunbathing?" Tan asked with a mischievous grin. "After those caves, you might enjoy Pangkor. It's a small, picturesque island that's only a short ferry ride from Lumut. But you can't take your car."

After finishing the mountains of food, everyone began to relax. The plump man put his hands across his stomach. Mustafa lit another cigar, and the other men did the same. Tan offered me a cigarette, but I declined. It already felt like I was sitting in a pea-soup London fog.

One of the younger men, called Anwar, asked whether I had a good road map. I said that it was in my car. He encouraged me to go get it, offering to advise me on which roads were the best to take. I thought this was a great idea, so I excused myself and went out to my car to fetch the map. It had been fun to have dinner with these kind and generous men, and now they were giving me some great travel tips. I felt incredibly lucky!

When I entered the restaurant with my map in hand, I was shocked to see that the table was empty. The men had disappeared. Was I dreaming? Had I just dined with nine men who had vanished into thin air? I was dumbfounded.

I looked around the restaurant and saw no one except for the approaching waiter, who had the bill in his hand.

"Where are all the men?" I asked.

"Gone," he replied.

"Gone?"

"Yes. And here's the bill." He shoved it into my outstretched hand.

I glanced at the bill. It was for over five hundred Malaysian ringgit! I felt the blood draining from my face as I tried to calculate how much this would be in Canadian dollars. I gripped a chair to steady myself when I realized that it was going to be a lot.

"I can't possibly afford this," I protested. I was trembling and on the verge of tears. "I'll pay for myself, but certainly *not* for the others."

"They told me you were going to pay," the waiter insisted.

"No," I argued. "I'm only going to pay for *my* portion of the meal." *Oh God*, I thought, *I'm going to end up in a Malaysian prison if I don't pay*.

I considered my options, but nothing rational came to mind. I knew that the hotel had an imprint of my credit card, so even if I didn't pay now they could charge me later. And I didn't have that kind of money to squander.

I tried to calm myself down, but I felt numb and confused. And outraged! I began to wonder if the men really did work for the Hong Kong Bank. I was furious with them, and furious with myself for being so trusting. I was a seasoned traveler, and I should have known better.

That's when I heard a loud cackle. I turned around and saw the nine men reappear from the direction of the kitchen. They were all laughing. Tan had taken off his glasses and was wiping tears from his eyes. Mustafa was doubled over, and the fat man was holding his shaking belly.

"You should have seen your face," Tan said, in between fits of laughter.

"Where were you?" I asked.

"Hiding in the stock room," said Anwar.

"And whose idea was this?" I demanded, still in shock.

"It was my idea," Tan admitted. He wore a boyish grin as he placed a comforting arm around my shoulder. The other men were still laughing.

After I had recovered from the scare, I too joined in. How could I not? These men had pulled the perfect practical joke, and they deserved some credit.

Eventually, after everyone had stopped laughing, I handed Anwar my map. "Now, will you please tell me where I need to go?"

For six years during the 1990s, Angela chaired the West End Writers' Club in Vancouver (now known as We Writers). It was there that she first had her creative non-fiction book critiqued—a book that she began in 1966 and is still working on. By some incredible coincidence, while Angela was on a South African safari in 2011, she met up with a Malaysian man who had worked with Tan at a bank in Kuala Lumpur.

Adventures with Reverend Lugio

A tireless man of the cloth, watching over his flock with 100-watt fog lights.

By Brent Curry

In the bicycle industry, there are many examples of socially conscious builders forging partnerships with ambitious and hardworking people in developing countries. Craig Calfee's work with Bamboosero, Tom Ritchey's work with Project Rwanda, and Ross Evans' work with Worldbike are nothing short of inspirational.

As the owner of The Bicycle Forest—a company that's engaged in the manufacture of quirky concept bicycles—I've often yearned for an opportunity to do my part. So when the chance to forge a partnership with an alleged former prime minister of Cameroon fell into my lap in 2009, I decided to investigate further.

Sadly, it turned out to be one of those Internet scams.

On May 19, 2010, I received another e-mail, this time from a humble church reverend from Kenya. Would this be my chance to make a difference in the world?

Dear Sir,

With much regards to your company services and products. I am Rev Lugio Ibrahim and would like to make a purchase on treadmill Best value for walking and some jogging. Kindly send me a return e-mail on what you currently have in stock and what you can offer with prices and availability.

God bless you
Rev. Lugio Ibrahim

Was this guy for real? Why would a church in Kenya order a treadmill from Canada? It didn't make sense. Unless, of course, he was placing an order for any random product and then scheming to pull an advance-fee fraud on the unsuspecting vendor.

As it happens, I was in a pretty good position to test the sanctity of my new acquaintance. You see, I don't sell treadmills. If a hasty Internet search had led him to believe that I did, that's only because I happen to advertise something similar but far more ridiculous: the "revolutionary" Treadmill Bike. If there's a more irresponsible way to invest the limited resources of a small church in Kenya than by purchasing a Treadmill Bike from Canada, I don't know what it is.

As a test, I responded to Reverend Lugio with an offer that would have been quite imprudent to accept.

Hello Reverend Lugio,

Thanks for writing. You can read all about our Treadmill Bike on our web site, bikeforest.com. It retails for $2,500. However, we are having a special on right now. If you purchase four Treadmill Bikes, we'll give you a fifth one for free.

Let me know if you are interested.
Brent

Sure enough, Reverend Lugio's next e-mail revealed his true colors:

Hello Brent,

Thank you for quote and please, I will like to order four Treadmill Bike and I want to know the total cost without shipping. for the pick up to enable us process freight and schedule pick up accordingly. so we can process payment. Kindly send total cost and what date it can pick up from your location?

Look forward to hear from you.

God bless you
Rev. Lugio Ibrahim

Since I knew at this point that Reverend Lugio was a scammer, I thought it would be interesting to see how much further I could string him along.

Hello Rev Lugio,

I'm sorry for the delayed response. Things have been quite busy here since we started our buy-four-get-one-free promotion.

The total cost for four Treadmill Bikes would be $10,000 Canadian. Of course, since you are buying four, you will actually get a fifth Treadmill Bike for free. I trust that you will still take the fifth bike even though it will likely increase your shipping costs.

I can have five Treadmill Bikes ready for pickup at our facility by Friday, June 18th. If you would like to pick up your order sooner, I have another shipment that was ready to go out last week, but wasn't shipped because there was a fire at the customer's warehouse and they needed to cancel the order at the last minute. This particular order is another five-Treadmill-Bike order, but it includes a couple of accessory packages.

One of the Treadmill Bikes is equipped with a dog-walking side attachment, while the other is equipped with a hot dog vending cart. I've attached photos of these accessory packages. Normally these two accessory packages would add an extra $3,700 to the cost. However, I will sell them to *you for only $1,500 extra. If you would like to proceed with this option, the total cost would be $11,500 and they could be picked up as early as tomorrow.*

Let me know which option you would prefer. Also, let me know your preferred method of payment.

Dog walking side attachment
Product code #45422
$800

Looking forward to hearing from you soon.

Brent

I have to admit, I was amused by Reverend Lugio's response.

Hotdog cart side attachment
Product code #45429
$2900

Hello Brent,

*Nice to hear from you again, the new total cost for $11,500
will be fine, since I need them earlier. please advice is asap
can I make payment with my master or visa credit card?*

Look forward to hear from you.

*God bless you
Rev. Lugio*

Lugio didn't seem fazed by the idea of a hot dog vending cart
attached to a treadmill on wheels. I figured that I might as well see
how much further I could pull the wool over his eyes.

Hello Rev. Lugio,

*I'm sorry for the delayed response. I have to apologize,
there was a miscommunication with our order fulfillment
department. The shipment that is available now does not
include the dog-walking attachment. Instead, it includes
the fog-walking accessory kit. The fog-walking accessory
kit is only $400 as opposed to $800 for the dog-walking
attachment. Therefore, the total cost for this order is only
$11,100. I trust that you will be okay with this. The fog-
walking accessory kit is our most popular option.*

I also neglected to mention that the hot dog vending cart comes with a complementary set of barbecue tongs. You can choose between cherry or ergo grip. Which would you prefer?

And yes, you can make payment with either Visa or Mastercard. When can we expect you to pick up this shipment? Let me know if there is anything more that I can do for you.

Looking forward to your response.
Brent

Fog walking accessory kit
Product code #45406
$400

I actually didn't hear back from Reverend Lugio, but on June 7th I was contacted by his associates at Globe Freight.

Dear Sir,

Thank you for choosing Globe Freight for your shipping needs. In regards to Lugio Ibrahim shipment. kindly forward detail requirement for the pick up. To enable us process freight and schedule pick up accordingly. Kindly send us the required info below.

1, pick up address
2, ship to address
3, Total weight of goods and dimension
4, Pick up date and time

Counting on your rapid correspondent to forward a quote and process pick up as requested.

Globe Freight
All ways at your service!!

General Manager
Benjamin Walter

This is how I responded:

Hello Benjamin,

Thanks for writing. I notice that Rev Lugio has been cc'd on this message. I trust that he received my earlier e-mail regarding the mix up about the fog-walking accessory kit. The shipment we have for him includes this accessory kit and not the dog-walking attachment. The cost of this shipment is therefore $11,100 instead of the originally quoted $11,500.

We also need to know Rev Lugio's preference for the complementary set of barbecue tongs. We have cherry or ergo grip. Please let us know your preference so that we can include these items in your shipment.

Here is the rest of the required information:

1. Pickup address is: ... Kitchener, Ontario, Canada
2. Ship to address: I do not know where Rev Lugio wants this shipment sent. Please check with him before pick-up.
3. Total weight: 835 lbs. Crate dimensions are 8' X 6' X 6'
4. Pickup date: We are open from 8am – 5pm, Monday to Friday. The shipment can be picked up anytime, but we would appreciate hearing from Rev Lugio regarding his barbecue tong preferences before releasing the shipment.

Please let me know if there is anything more I can do to help. Looking forward to hearing back from Rev Lugio about the barbecue tongs and shipping destination.

Brent

The next day, I heard from Reverend Lugio.

Hello Brent,

Thank you for the details, please send me your phone. I would like to make the payment with my credit card on Phone and concerning the barbecue tong what are the prices and do you have it in stock?

Waiting for your urgent response.

God bless you
Rev. Lugio

Hello Rev Lugio,

The barbecue tongs are complementary. They are included with the hot dog vending cart attachment. If you would like to purchase additional tongs, they are sold individually for $10, or $400 for a box of fifty. They come in cherry or ergo grip. Both are the same price and we have plenty of each.

Please let me know your preference for your complementary pair, and also whether or not you'd like to purchase additional boxes.

At the Bicycle Forest, we pride ourselves on our commitment to customer service. I must insist that I pay for the phone charges when accepting your credit card number. Please send me your phone number and I'll call you later today.

Brent

Hello Brent,

I will order 50 boxes for the cherry and 50 boxes for ergo grip. making 40 boxes. Kindly send the rest of the details to my shipping company I would like to know how much I will spend on transporting shipment to my church in Kenya -Nairobi. You can also reach me on 339 368 6907.

Waiting for your urgent response.

God bless you
Rev. Lugio

I had a brief phone conversation with Lugio. There was a fair bit of confusion on both ends concerning the number of barbecue tongs he wanted to purchase with the order, but we got that sorted out. I think we were both relieved to hang up the phone and resume our e-mail communication.

Hello Benjamin,

I was speaking on the phone with Rev Lugio today. He said he would e-mail me his shipping address, but I have yet to receive that from him. I've cc'd Rev Lugio on this e-mail in the hopes that he will let us both know the address ASAP. He did say that the shipment would be going to Nairobi, Kenya though.

It turns out that I will be including two additional boxes of barbecue tongs with the shipment. Each box is 2' X 2' X 2'. When I add these boxes to the crate, there is still some empty space that would really be worth filling with something. I would recommend adding two Teenage Mutant Ninja Turtles inflatable swimming pools to the order. This product ships in a 6' X 3' X 2' box and is currently on clearance for only $150. If you purchase these products, I'll include a third box of barbecue tongs at half price. This will fill the remaining 2' X 2' X 2' gap in the crate. Rev Lugio, if this is acceptable to you, then the dimensions of your shipping crate will be 8' X 8' X 6'. The total weight will be 962 lbs. The total cost will be $12,400.

Benjamin, I hope that Rev Lugio will forward you his shipping address post-haste. If there is anything more I can do for either of you, please don't hesitate to let me know.

Brent

Hello Brent,

Yes please include Teenage Mutant Ninja Turtles inflatable swimming pools. Moreover the ship to address is below.

Rev Samuel Dean
Church of Christ
5th beauty St
Nairobi, Kenya
233540896652

I will call you early morning to make payment to enable pick up take place. God bless you and looking forward to make business with you in the near future!!

Rev. Lugio

After a bit of back and forth with the boys at Globe Freight, I received the following e-mail summary on June 9th:

Dear Valued Customer,

Thank you for your co-operation the estimate cost for the shipping will sum up $5,950 this includes Air freight charges, tax, packaging, insurance and 3day delivery service as advice by Rev Lugio Ibrahim.

We don't have credit card facilities to process credit card payment. However we require payment via money gram for overseas shipment to proceed with packaging.

Upon receipt of payment info from money gram or western union we will forward you a representative for packaging and pick up.

For overseas shipment please make payment via money Gram to the Account Manager West/Africa department. Please send payment details to update your pick up details in our data system before packaging and pick up.

Yahaya Samba
5th airport st
cantonment
Accra-Ghana,
23324
tel:233248833316

Globe Freight
All ways at your call!!
Benjamin

Later that day I got a phone call from Reverend Lugio. As promised, he wanted to cover the shipping costs himself. Unfortunately, he claimed not to have the ability to pay by MoneyGram. He instead proposed that I pay the fees by MoneyGram myself, and in turn charge his credit card the same amount. He proceeded to dictate a credit card number over the phone. Having no intention of charging the card, I didn't even write the number down. After pretending to ring up the sale, I told him that the card had been declined. To this, he asked me to repeat the number to make sure that I had got it correct. Of course, I had no clue what the number was, so I just rhymed off a bunch of digits. He soon cut me off. Apologizing, he said he likely wasn't speaking clearly enough. We tried it again and this time I wrote down the number. Of course, I still didn't plan to do anything with it, and once again I told him it was declined. He tried again with two other numbers, but my response was always the same.

At this point, I couldn't help but ask what he intended to do at his church with five Treadmill Bikes, one equipped with high-powered fog lights and the other outfitted with a hot dog vending cart, as well as 150 barbecue tongs and two Teenage Mutant Ninja Turtles inflatable swimming pools. To this, he said that he intended to offer them as prizes in a fundraising raffle.

I soon received yet another e-mail from Reverend Lugio.

Hello Brent,

Thank you for spending time on the phone, I sometimes have sight problem, I would like to provide you with the credit card details via email. please split total cost of order plus shipping equally among the, master credit card details below bit by bit.

(Reverend Lugio listed the credit card details of two random people, but for obvious reasons, I'm not going to reprint them.)

Look forward to hear from you.

God bless you
Rev. Lugio

Sadly, I've been left lacking proper closure to this story. I wrote back to Reverend Lugio with the sad news that the other credit cards to which he hoped to charge a total of $5,950 were also declined. I suggested that he forward me some information about his church and the plans he had for the five treadmill bikes, fog lights, hot dog vending cart, 150 barbecue tongs and two Teenage Mutant Ninja Turtles inflatable swimming pools. I realize there was talk of a raffle, but I know that his full plan would have been so much more than that. I figured we just had to get the word out about his project and people would get behind Reverend Lugio with the financial support he so desperately needed.

I can hear the clasps of those wallets and change purses opening already. But alas, it's too late. I have not heard from Reverend Lugio now for over a year. Nevertheless, he lives on in my heart. Although we've never met, I can see him perfectly: a tireless man of the cloth, watching over his flock by night aboard a treadmill bike outfitted with 100-watt fog lights.

With Reverend Lugio as my shepherd, I shall not want.

Brent Curry owns a business called The Bicycle Forest, *which promotes the use of bicycles and other human-powered vehicles as a viable form of transportation. Brent also enjoys the occasional e-mail exchange with Internet scammers. One of Brent's other virtual adventures involved him negotiating a twelve-million-dollar contract for 50,000 comfort bicycles with an alleged former prime minister of Cameroon. He also facilitated a multimillion-dollar investment opportunity with a former government official from Ghana, while at the same time riding a pedal-powered pickup truck filled with pancake mix across Canada. You can visit Brent at his company's web site: www.bikeforest.com.*

The Turkish Bath

Woman with moustache is one scary lady...

By Heather Lea

On a fall evening in 2007, while the leaves in Canada were turning, I was getting my bare backside slapped by a woman with a moustache in Istanbul.

I was fresh from a seventy-two-day bike tour, during which five friends and I had cycled from Paris to Istanbul. It's not surprising that a Turkish bath seemed like a great idea.

It wasn't.

The owner of my hostel divulged the location of a non-touristy bath in the area. His directions led us through secretive streets and eventually to the building itself, which looked seedy and rundown. I thought about leaving, but was committed by curiosity and walked in against my better judgment.

An old woman with a unibrow approached and showed me to a changing room where some well-worn flip-flops and a tatty looking towel awaited.

In the main bathing area, steamy shafts of light filtered through cracks in the steeple above. The room was muggy and claustrophobic. A dripping sound came from the urinal-like urns mounted to the walls. The old woman turned and revealed a beard, which reminded me of burned trees in a sparse forest. She barked "*Vash!*" gestured to the urns, and left.

I took a plastic bowl from beside one of the urns and began splashing water over myself, assuming that this was what she meant by "*Vash!*" Several minutes passed. Feeling modest, I tried to cover myself with my hands while watching a local woman across the room. She seemed to be enjoying herself thoroughly and barely noticed me until, unsure of what to do next, I headed for the door. She looked up and said, "Finish?"

Wrapped in the thin towel, I went back out into the foyer. I could feel the rubber sandals flicking stuff up onto my legs.

There was a shocked murmuring when I emerged. The old lady waddled over and more or less pushed me back into the bathroom. Again she growled, "*Vash!*"

Maybe this was a Turkish prison…

Back in the room with dense, moist air, I splashed bowl after bowl of water over myself. To say that I was feeling uncomfortable is an understatement.

The old lady finally came back. But her appearance did little to calm my nerves. She was now naked, except for a black pair of bikini underwear.

All I could think was: *Please don't be my masseuse!*

She summoned me by slapping her hand on a giant slab of marble. When I approached, she forced me down onto my back and began a vigorous rubdown with a sponge that looked like a wire pot cleaner.

With some kind of Judo maneuver, I was suddenly flipped over and positioned facedown on the wet marble. Another vigorous rubdown ensued, accompanied by a slap on the backside.

What was with all this slapping?

She directed me to "*Vash!*" again, and I had the pleasure of sitting where others and their "parts" had sat before me.

Then came the familiar slap on the marble—my cue.

When I approached, I was relieved to see a bar of soap. The old lady went hard at scrubbing my arms. I watched, embarrassed, as my limp hands slapped against her long, sagging breasts while she worked. Averting my attention, I was astonished to see gloppy balls of dead skin forming all over my arms. Disgusting! But somehow also fascinating...

Eventually, so much lather formed that her attempts to manhandle me around the slab were akin to using bare hands to catch a fish. A breaking point was reached, and I heard great, gulping sobs of my own laughter.

She slapped my backside again. "*Vash!*" she commanded.

There was a shampoo session next. She placed my face between her breasts and scrubbed away at my scalp. I had trouble breathing, until she mercifully pulled my head back, and with a resounding *shhhlock!* the seal was broken. Once again, air filled my lungs.

Then, by the grace of almighty God, it was over. In the changing room, I gingerly eased into my clothes, raw and stinging. At the cash register, she came over sporting a smile. Hovering at my shoulders, she gestured to my wallet. I was still coherent enough to understand that I should give her a tip. I did—because I was terrified to imagine what torture she reserves for non-tippers.

Heather Lea loves traveling, drinking wine and listening to good adventure stories—in that order. She has written for various outdoor magazines, including Gripped, Climbing, The Canadian Alpine Journal *and* Kootenay Mountain Culture. *In 2005 she founded an Arts, Culture and Lifestyles magazine called* Reved Quarterly (www.reved.net), *which is published independently out of Revelstoke, BC. Heather now lives in Vancouver, where she runs her multimedia company,* Reved Media and Design.

Purple and Green

Yes, I drank out of the red cup!

By Matt Hill

"Vanessa, did you put hot sauce and oranges in this or something?" I asked after downing the last drops of my protein replenishment drink. I was puzzled because it usually tasted like chocolate and blueberries. All I could taste this time was burnt oranges. And my stomach was starting to heat up.

"You didn't just drink from that red cup, did you?" she asked anxiously.

"Yes..."

"The red cup that was right beside the blender?"

"Yes..."

"That red cup that was *right* beside the blender?" she asked again, as if emphasizing a single word would elicit a different response.

"Yes. The red cup *right* beside the blender. I always drink my protein shakes from it."

Vanessa's eyes went wide. She sprinted to the RV's cubicle-like bathroom and looked inside. She pulled her head back out and went suddenly silent. I could see color draining from her face.

She asked me again, speaking now in a cautious, even tempo. "You drank from the red cup that was *right* beside the blender...?"

"Yes! I did!" I exclaimed. She was starting to freak me out. "I *always* drink from that cup. Ever since Day One of this running tour!"

"OH NO! OH NO! OH NO!"

*   *   *

It would be fair to say that this was not the first miscue on our Run for One Planet tour. Things don't always go as planned when you're running around a continent.

When my partner Stephanie Tait and I were training for our epic run, we knew that we might be putting ourselves in harm's way. Not only would we be at the mercy of speeding cars and trucks—and reckless drivers—along the highways, but there would be the daily wear and tear on our bodies as we ran across Canada, down the Eastern Seaboard to Florida, across the southern United States, and then back up the West Coast to Vancouver. There's not much that can prepare you for two hundred and twenty marathons in a single year.

Considering the many dangers and hardships we knew we would face, we had even agreed before the run that if one of us made the "Big Run up the Heaven" prematurely, the other would continue until the project was finished.

And it was important to us that we finished. The run wasn't just about challenging ourselves. In fact, we weren't doing it for us at all, because Steph really doesn't *like* running all that much. We were doing it because we are deeply concerned about the future of our planet, and we wanted to use the run as a platform for spreading the message of building a sustainable future. We planned to talk to the media in the cities we ran through; we organized dozens of environmental action events; and we visited hundreds of schools along our route to talk to children about things we can do in our lives to reduce our impact on the planet. It was intoxicating to meet so many enthusiastic kids. We heard countless stories of them creating change by discussing our ideas with adults in a kind of "trickle up" effect, and it soon became obvious that they were our secret weapon. We dubbed them our "pint-sized eco-warriors."

Maybe that's why we felt so attached to the dream of running around North America. It felt like we were doing something that was bigger than ourselves.

But back to the challenges, as there were plenty of them.

The first one was a landslide in Roger's Pass that closed the Trans-Canada Highway just a few days after we left Vancouver. The landslide blocked the highway for two long days, meaning that we were behind schedule almost immediately. This wouldn't have been a problem except for the dozens of public events and media interviews my cousin Vanessa (our RV driver and tour manager) had booked for us weeks in advance. This meant that to get back on schedule while running across the Canadian Prairies, Steph and I had been forced to suck up the pain and run ten marathons in seven days to reach Winnipeg on time. We got there with an hour to spare, passed out for fifteen minutes, then put on clean T-shirts and deodorant and met a Winnipeg running group for another ten-kilometer run.

Then there was northern Ontario: blackfly and mosquito hell. It was bad enough running with buzzing insects around our heads during the day. But even our touring RV—which we nicknamed

Racy Verna—provided little refuge at night. Somehow the biting insects found their way inside, and on several mornings we awoke covered in blood.

In southern Ontario, the arches on Steph's feet collapsed. Plagued by an ankle injury she had sustained at the beginning of the tour—when she had sprinted up a thousand feet of elevation in the Canadian Rockies—Steph's calf muscles quit on her. Every time she took a step, it felt like a nail was jabbing her in the foot.

To add insult to injury, her body had also started rejecting the iron supplements she was taking in order to keep her energy levels up. Our chiropractor, Don, called the attractive side effect "Purple Teeth Syndrome." At first it merely looked like she had been eating too many blueberries or drinking too much grape juice. Every time she smiled, it parted the curtains on a set of purple Chiclets. As time progressed, however, and she ran further and further on the injury (while her body continued to reject more and more iron), her teeth became increasingly darker shades of purple. It wasn't long before her infectious smile—with her normally perfect white teeth—had been replaced by a set of Cinderella's ugly-stepsister molars.

Despite all these hardships, I couldn't have predicted what would happen in Quebec.

When you are running four marathons (or more) every week, your body uses a lot of calories. And my blueberry chocolate protein shakes had become the stuff of legend on the Run for One Planet tour. It was easy to recognize when I needed one: the primary symptom was a glassy, confused stare, coupled with an inability to speak full and audible sentences. The same went for Steph, only she was always brought back to life with a large helping of Brie cheese and a box of crackers.

I always drank my beloved shake out of one of our many red cups, which always sat beside the blender on the kitchen counter.

Always.

Well—always, apparently, except for that particular day.

When I crawled into the RV with glazed-over eyes, looking for my lifesaver of a protein shake in my prized red cup, I mumbled something like, "Need shake ... food now ... going down ... hungry."

Vanessa tersely replied, "I made it already. It's in the blender."

I assumed that the fluid in the red cup *beside* the blender was my protein shake, ready to go. And in my calorie-depleted state, I chugged it.

"Eww, gross, Vanessa. This tastes disgusting!"

"Just drink it," she shot back in a tone that implied, "I'm busy and tired, too." She and Steph had been working for the last few hours on our complicated tour logistics.

Steph added from her side of their work table, "Yeah, Matt, just drink it."

They both snickered in that "girls gotta stick together" manner. I understood the rules. I was the only boy in the clubhouse at that moment. So I shrugged and downed the rest of the vile concoction.

*   *   *

"Vanessa, did you put hot sauce and oranges in this or something? My protein shake tastes like burnt oranges, and my stomach is getting really warm."

This last remark instantly got Vanessa's attention. She looked up and asked me the series of "red cup" questions. Cut back to her sprinting to the bathroom, culminating in her response: "OH NO! OH NO! OH NO!"

She grabbed the now empty red cup from my trembling hands, hurried back into the bathroom, let out a scream, and ran back to me with a bottle in her hands.

"You just drank an entire bottle of bathroom cleaner!" she cried.

In a high-pitched voice, she continued, "I was cleaning the bathroom and couldn't find a cup. So I grabbed the red cup beside the blender and used that. I forgot to put it in the sink before making your protein shake!"

By now, sweat was cascading down my face like a storm-swollen river. In my completely exhausted and calorie-depleted state, the first question that raced through my mind was: "Am I going to die in a province where I don't even speak the language?!"

Would my gravestone read:

RIP MONSIEUR MATT

Died after drinking an entire bottle of bathroom cleanser while running around North America with purple-toothed run partner.

All written in French, of course!

Steph sprang into action and grabbed the empty cleanser bottle from Vanessa's shaking hands. She was the only calm one among us, and also the only one who could read the French label.

She skimmed down the bottle. For some reason, among paragraphs written in French, there was a single sentence in English. Written in large black letters, it read: IF INGESTED, SEEK IMMEDIATE MEDICAL ATTENTION.

At this point, it took us a little longer to digest the information. We read that sentence over several times, staring at it for what felt like eternity. All at once, we understood what it meant, and that this wasn't some kind of joke. This was real, and we needed to seek immediate medical attention … *immediately!*

I completely freaked out. I began screaming, "I'm going to die! I'm going to die!"

Steph's usually unruffled demeanor turned slightly ruffled as she tried to calm me down.

Vanessa jumped into the driver's seat, started the engine, and pulled onto the highway. Steph turned on our GPS unit— Belinda—to locate the nearest hospital. I continued to sweat profusely, downing copious amounts of water to quench my burnt-orange-tasting mouth and cool my now very warm stomach.

A new and unwelcome symptom appeared: gas fumes. And I'm not talking about fumes trailing from the tailpipe of our RV. Picture a 28-foot RV with Run for One Planet logos on the outside and copious amounts of Matt-gas on the inside, speeding down the peaceful streets of a little French village called St. Antoine in desperate search of a hospital.

Luckily for us, hospitals have the universal H sign to guide distressed folks like us to safety. When we spotted that H, Vanessa cranked the wheel hard to the left and barely made the turn into the parking lot. For added effect, "Belinda" offered her computer-generated opinion that we were "off route," confused because Vanessa had entered the hospital's parking lot through the back entrance. Vanessa pulled up in front of the big red Emergency doors like a SWAT team arriving at a bank robbery.

Steph and I jumped out and raced inside to find a doctor. We rushed toward the front desk attendant, who was—fortunately for her—protected by a glass window. When she looked up and saw Steph's purple teeth and my terrified face, you'd imagine she might panic. But she calmly instructed us to sit down and wait for the next physician.

I'll be the first to admit that I was in full panic mode by now. In a desperate attempt to cut the line, I babbled the whole story to her: running around North America, extra mileage, my red cup, the bathroom cleaner, the whole nine yards. After patiently waiting for me to complete my panicky monologue, she responded in French. I couldn't understand a word she said, which may have been a smart strategy on her part to get me to sit down and leave her alone.

After what felt like an eternity (i.e., likely two or three minutes), we were escorted into an examination room to await the doctor who, I was now convinced, was going to need to pump my stomach.

After what felt like another eternity (i.e., another two or three minutes), a doctor appeared and suggested in French that we should follow him. Fortunately, Steph is fluent in French and was easily able to converse with the physician.

Their conversation went like this:

"Blah, blah, blah, blah," said Steph in French.

"Blah, blah, blah, blah," replied the doctor.

Both of them looked over at me. I saw Steph mime the action of drinking, followed by my disgusted reaction to the taste.

And their incomprehensible dialogue continued.

"Blah, blah, blah, blah," said Steph.

"Blah, blah, blah, blah," replied the doctor.

I felt a bit calmer knowing that Steph was giving him very detailed information. Yet I wasn't getting any confirmation from their facial expressions that everything was going to be alright. In fact, I saw in their eyes what appeared to be deep concern. They started miming the action of stomach pumping, throwing up, and putting a needle into my arm.

That's it, I thought. I'm going to die right here and now.

Their conversation seemed to go back and forth for what seemed like a lifetime (i.e., another two or three minutes). I began writing an obituary in my mind, with clear instructions that would instruct Steph to escort my corpse back to Vancouver for a proper English burial before completing the tour.

As I was finishing the preparations for my own funeral, the dire-sounding conversation finished with both of them giggling. Then they turned to look at me with what I can only describe as looks of compassion.

I knew it. They were going to let me down easy. We obviously hadn't sought IMMEDIATE MEDICAL ATTENTION immediately enough. Blame it on Belinda.

But why wasn't Steph crying? Wasn't she going to miss me?

The doctor gave Steph a kiss on both cheeks, gave me the thumbs-up signal, and calmly walked out the door.

"What on earth is going on?" I asked Steph. I was utterly confused, and became even more so when Steph began walking toward the door.

"Let's go," she said. "You're going to be fine."

"What do you mean I'm going to be fine?"

She stopped and looked up at me. I could see that she was trying hard not to laugh. Then, speaking slowly and simply as though giving instructions to a confused child, she explained the situation. Basically, given the nature of our tour and the message of sustainability we were spreading, we had diligently purchased an earth-friendly green cleaner whose ingredients were natural plant extracts and fruit enzymes (hence the distinct burnt-orange taste).

In my delusional state, I had overlooked the fact that I had drunk a green cleaner cocktail that didn't contain any toxic ingredients like bleach or ammonia, as many other cleaning products do. These chemicals are harmful not only to the earth, but also to people's health if they're ingested. Green cleaners, on the other hand, dilute naturally in water and leave no trace behind.

Well, that's not entirely true. The doctor *had* mentioned that I might have some diarrhea.

And what were the stomach-pumping, retching, and needle-in-the-arm gestures all about? With a big, purple grin, Steph shared that—once she knew I was going to be alright—she had figured she would let the joke run its course just a little bit longer.

With the three of us living in a 28-foot RV, on a tight schedule and with lots of demands on our time, sometimes a little humor is called for.

As it turned out, the French doctor was right about my body's natural process of getting rid of the green cleaner. Let's just say the payback on Steph and her practical joke didn't smell too sweet after a good joke on me. On the other hand, I still had six miles to run, and in my opinion the fresh outdoor air smelled just fine.

If there's a moral to this story, I like to think it's this: use green cleaners. The health of the planet (and possibly *your* own health) might one day depend on it.

Matt Hill launched his acting career at the age of fifteen, when he landed a role standing next to his childhood crush, Lindsey Wagner, the Bionic Woman. He has since played Jackie Chan's deputy in Shanghai Knights, *a whacked-out Vietnam vet in Steven Spielberg's mini series* Taken, *and was the voice of Raphael in the* Teenage Mutant Ninja Turtles III, *among many other roles. During this time, Matt has never stopped running. At last count he has completed close to three hundred marathons, and has crossed the Ironman finish line seven times. In 2006, along with his friend and running partner Stephanie Tait, Matt founded* Run for One Planet *(www.runforoneplanet.com), an organization designed to educate kids on issues of sustainability and inspire environmental action.*

Jumping the Bull

Little white lies that lead to marriage proposals.

By Maureen Magee

I tell lies when I travel. My mother would call them "little white lies"—and I only tell them to spare the feelings of others.

Oh, all right. That isn't exactly honest. I tell lies when I travel in order to spare *myself* the piteous looks I receive when I tell the truth. A woman traveling alone is not as rare a thing as it once was, but—depending on where she goes—there is still a curiosity factor. The farther afield she wanders, the more curious the local folks will be.

"Where is your husband?" That is the first question.

Now, I never mind admitting that I am single—I am an optimist, and the inquirer just might have some terrific friend I could meet. Of course, if I answer truthfully and admit to two divorces, I could appear to be a poor risk. So I hang my head, and in a tragic voice, I whisper, "Gone."

Which is not a lie. Not really. They *are* all gone, those husbands.

"Do you have children?"

To tell the truth, I am not a talented liar, and this next question is where the real lie occurs. I am a blissfully child-free woman. So many cultures adore children and consider them one of the world's greatest blessings. By acknowledging that I have no kids, I am faced with astonishment, sorrow, advice, and the offer of prayers, herbs, or incense to correct the situation.

Believe me, I have tried to be up front and explain the freedom of choice we have in North America. But whether I am on Baffin Island or in Bali, in the Omo Valley or in Otovalo, I only sadden or confuse the curious.

Honestly, it seems almost necessary to lie.

I pull out a photograph of two boys and a girl, all adorable. As I show the picture, I gaze lovingly at it and accept compliments. I found the photograph stuck in a book I bought from a thrift store. It is starting to look a little old and tatty now, and I might have to find a new one. As a matter of fact, *I* am also looking older and tattier, and perhaps should be claiming them as grandchildren.

This technique worked well for years until that one day in a remote corner of exotic Ethiopia—the day I forgot to lie. Not only did the truth almost do me in, but I met my match in facile fibbing…

I was on my first visit to Ethiopia, for the filming of a travel documentary series. We were visiting the various tribal cultures of the Omo Valley and had set up our campsite near the tiny town of Turmi, close to where the semi-nomadic Hamer tribe scattered themselves. A handsome young Hamer man named Kelile had found us, and because he spoke some English, we hired him as a guide while we wandered through his remote hamlet.

Kelile was about twenty years old; he wore the traditional sarong-type skirt with an old T-shirt advertising a chic Paris hotel. During one of the filming breaks, Kelile caught me off guard by skipping the usual first question and proceeding straight to the second.

"Do you have children?" he asked.

"Oh good grief, no!" I replied without thinking.

Oops.

His lovely brown doe-eyes saddened as he absorbed this. He remained quiet. Then he seemed to make a decision. He gently put his hand on my arm, looked straight into my eyes, and said, "Next month I am jumping the bull." He nodded encouragingly at my blank face.

"You're *what?*"

"I am JUMPING THE BULL," he replied in a deliberate voice, as if slowing down the delivery of the words would help me to understand. His eyes had locked onto mine and he nodded again, more forcibly.

I nodded back, smiling vaguely.

He looked frustrated. I knew how he felt—I hadn't a clue what he was going on about.

He took a deep breath. "After I jump the bull, then I can give you babies."

Oh, dear. My head was a jumble of manic thoughts: bulls = penises + tribal men from strange cultures + doing things with bulls = getting me pregnant + how could *that be?* + *why* had I ever come here? + where exactly *was* here...?

I looked around in a panic for our guide Mageru, who during this trip had solved many problems. I waved him over with the traditional Ethiopian upside-down finger waggling and incoherently whispered a summary of the situation.

Mageru swallowed a smile. He punched Kelile playfully in the shoulder and shook his hand.

I was not reassured.

They chatted in Amharic with Mageru growing more serious. Kelile raised his eyebrows and looked sheepish. Mageru patted me on the shoulder in an "everything is fine" manner and wandered off.

It was a mystery.

We finished our filming, shook hands with Kelile, and said goodbye. All seemed normal. On the drive back to the campsite, I grilled Mageru.

"What was that all about?"

"The young Hamer men have a rite of passage in order to prove themselves worthy of being married. All the cattle of the village are lined up side by side. The man must strip naked, take a running leap, and race across the backs of the animals. If he can do it four times without falling, he can take a wife. If not, he must wait another year."

"So he was proposing to me?"

Mageru nodded.

"But what made him stop talking about it? What did you say?"

"I told him you were my girlfriend."

"You WHAT?" I stammered. "But ... THAT'S A LIE!"

Epilogue:

Six months after this tale took place, Maureen Elizabeth Magee married her guide Mageru. They did not have babies. No bulls were involved. Honest.

Maureen Magee is a Calgary-based travel writer who began traveling as a five-star butterfly, flitting lightly through distant lands and cultures. While pleasant, this required financing beyond her means, and so—defying her own nature—she metamorphosed backwards into a down-and-dirty caterpillar. She now slugs her way around the world in a far less fashionable, but infinitely more enjoyable style.

Four Dollars and a Microwave

Sometimes a story is worth pursuing for its own sake.

By Kyle MacDonald

Whether you budget wisely or throw caution to the wind, when you travel the cash eventually runs out. You reach a point when you're pretty much willing to accept any job or do anything, as long as it buys food and pays the bills.

My wallet bottomed out in Montreal, where my girlfriend and I had hoped to try living for a while. She had already found a job, and now it was my turn to find something to pull in my share of the rent. And while I'll be the first to admit that pulling in minimum wage to hand out promotional flyers at a metro station wasn't the type of post-university career I had in mind, I comforted myself with the thought that it was a "travel experience." Besides, something better would certainly come along soon.

I entered the station and decided that the enclave at the top of the escalators was the spot to maximize on passersby. The perturbed glare from the *Watchtower* pusher who arrived moments after I did confirmed my suspicions. This was *the* spot.

When you enter university, you don't visualize yourself doing something like this upon graduation—that is, frequenting public transit facilities in order to compete with middle-aged Jehovah's

Witnesses for the best place to distribute promotional literature. If only they could see me now, the dozens of people who'd had the nerve to question: "What do you plan to do with a bachelor's degree in *geography?*" I realized that my skills for picking out a good location were being unceremoniously wasted. I made a mental note to find a better form of employment. Correction: I made a mental note to find any other form of employment. While debating in my mind whether owning a hot dog stand or ice cream truck would be a more profitable venture, a man with an East Indian accent approached me and pointed at my stack of flyers.

"Are you having a job?" he asked.

"Pardon?"

"Are you working?"

"Uh, yes. I'm working right now if that's what you're asking."

"I see," he said. "You are already having a job. I am looking for somebody who needs a job."

"Well I kinda have this flyer thing going on right now. It's only a short contract though, and today is my last day."

"Can you fold things?"

"Yeah, sure. Why?"

"I have a job for somebody who can do folding."

"I'll be done with this at ten o'clock," I said hopefully.

"Here is my phone number. Be calling me at ten o'clock. I am Sasha. You will work for me. You will do folding."

When you're standing at a metro station pondering employment opportunities, and a sketchy guy offers you a job, you're either going to land a good job or a good story. Today was going to be a surefire winner. I could just feel it.

By five after ten, I found myself in the passenger seat of a 1991 Dodge Caravan equipped with shiny running boards and dark-tinted windows. "This is good van. Dodge. I am selling it. You might want this van. Two thousand and five hundred. Good price, my friend."

We commenced making the rounds of Sasha's neighborhood by searching for the elusive store-owner-lady who hadn't paid him for her last order of T-shirts: "She's not selling my shirts again. She is a bad lady. She doesn't be selling anything for me."

Then we knocked on the door of an obviously closed and deserted restaurant, apparently owned by his brother. He turned to me and said: "There is a job in this restaurant for you if you be wanting it."

By this point I'd taken a liking to Sasha. His unorthodox entrepreneurial style was interesting, to say the least, and I was curious to learn more about the promised "folding" activity. It took Sasha ten minutes to drive from the metro station to what seemed like another continent. It may have been the basement of a modest house in the north end of Montreal, but from my knowledge of international workplace safety standards cultivated from a lifetime of reading National Geographic magazine, I may as well have been in India.

The basement was a scene of disarray rivaled only by a Calcutta garment factory. Boxes were piled to the top of the seven-foot-high ceilings, and I could see several spliced electrical cords and ramshackle sewing machines. It was a basement sweatshop—plain and simple. Still unsure of the legitimacy of his business, I searched but could not find the two elements that could have proven it illegal: labor exploitation and/or a smoldering fire hazard.

"I have plastic for you to fold," said Sasha.

It sounded easy. Like every other kid in grade eight who owned a Bic pen, I learned how to fold plastic the first day our science teacher let us use the Bunsen burners. The premise is simple: you heat the plastic until it's soft, then you bend it. As it turned out, rather than make a costly purchase, Sasha had invented his own electric folding machine. A car-battery charger was plugged into the wall socket and its live leads were placed on a nearby table. However, instead of attaching the live leads to a dead car battery, as is the usual style, Sasha had ingeniously attached them to a pair of nails connected by a thin piece of wire. As the current began to flow, the wire quickly became red hot. To add danger to the beauty of his contraption, the entire heat-producing assembly was mounted to a piece of wood, which began to smolder.

Why buy a safe product when there are plenty of capable firefighters in the city? I thought to myself.

After showing me how it worked, Sasha looked at me with a dead-serious expression on his face: "Do not tell *anybody* that you are working for me. OK, we be starting now."

As promised, my job description *was* simple. I was there to fold. Sasha instructed me to fold four-inch pieces of paper-thin transparent plastic into what looked like name-badge holders. Held over the radiant wire, the plastic became quite malleable, and with two quick folds, the square pieces were able to hold paper badges. After forty-five seconds of training, Sasha felt that I was capable of working alone.

"If you are leaving, turn electricity off. We don't want be wasting money on electricity."

Or to turn the building into a pile of cinders and ash, I thought.

Feeling productive, I managed to find a rhythm and was well on my way to becoming the best illegal-basement-plastic-badge-bender in all of Eastern Canada. After an hour, I stood proudly over two hundred completed name badges. Sasha strolled downstairs with a coffee in hand, sized up my output, and put me in my place. "You are too slow. My child is faster than you. He is seven. Maybe one day you will be good."

He grabbed a piece of plastic and showed me his technique. "Do like this ... softly. Yes, this is better. For each bundle of one hundred pieces I will be giving you one dollar."

Possibly because I was still in shock over the myriad of workplace safety, tax, and labor laws being broken, the economic reality of Sasha's statement didn't immediately sink in. Perhaps the fumes from the melting plastic and the smoldering wood had put me in an inebriated state. Through the fog, I began to crunch the numbers. I calculated that being paid one dollar for every one hundred pieces was going to net me two dollars per hour at my current rate. Being currently jobless and with nothing else better to do—or perhaps more accurately, nothing worse to do—I decided to continue. The only thought that entered my plastic-fume-riddled brain was: *I'll just keep at this until I get a free lunch.*

After another hour at a similar pace, I had amassed a pile of four hundred badge holders. Good enough to buy my freedom with a four-dollar lunch.

Being a savvy businessman, Sasha sensed the onset of lunchtime hunger and began promoting his post-lunchtime work opportunities. "I have many jobs for you," he said. "Painting is one of these jobs. Twenty dollars each room. I also have many things for sale to my friends. Would you be needing a couch, bed, television, microwave?"

Funnily enough, a microwave was something I could use. I had been putting off buying a microwave until the right deal came along. Clearly, this was the deal I'd been waiting for.

"How much do you want for the microwave?"

"Ten dollars."

"Ten bucks," I said thoughtfully, weighing my options.

It was a low price, all things considered. But I had only four dollars' worth of work under my belt. I was out of cash, so unless Sasha accepted Visa, I would have to work another three hours at my current pace to earn enough for the microwave. And I hadn't remembered seeing an "Accepted here: VISA" sticker on the front window of his house, so I scratched my head and considered whether I could stomach another three hours of plastic fumes.

Sasha must have seen the look of concern on my face and realized that he would lose any chance of my returning to his "factory" if he didn't act quickly to sweeten the deal.

"Okay, ten dollars for normally, but for you my friend: no price. Free."

OK. Time out. Imagine it's the mid-1940s and we're inside the laboratory of a scientist who is designing the world's very first microwave. Imagine what his prediction might be for this cutting-edge technology:

Microwave technology will be expensive at first. But it will revolutionize the way housewives cook their meals. Never again will they face the rigors of slaving over a hot stove all day long. Being an advanced food-warming technology, it will be an appliance for the rich to begin with. But over time the cost of a microwave oven will drop steadily. By the start of the 21st century, microwave ovens might even be the preferred currency for sweatshop proprietors employing illegal laborers in their basement firetraps.

Minutes later, I found myself walking down the street waving goodbye to Sasha. I had four dollars in one hand and a microwave in the other. My lunch? A pair of microwaveable frozen burritos.

And that's how you earn four dollars and a microwave in Montreal.

Epilogue:

Since it wasn't hot enough outside that day, and because the red-hot plastic-bender did not produce enough BTUs for me to actually break a sweat, I have not yet been able to claim that I've worked in a bona fide sweatshop.

All a university graduate can do is dream.

Kyle MacDonald is a public speaker and world-record holder who loves traveling as much as he enjoys watching videos of cats on the Internet. He once traded a red paperclip for a house to much fanfare. His mom still cuts his hair.

Cornbread and Wolverines

What are the chances of that happening?

By Tim Irvin

Traveling alone by canoe for forty-five days is worth it, if only to taste fresh cornbread on day thirty-two.

This was what I had been thinking about the day I saw the wolverine.

Drifting mid-river, savoring the fresh cornbread I had baked that morning, I was deep in the throes of what my Dad used to call a gastric orgasm. Somewhere downstream, a wolverine was nosing its way in my direction. But I didn't know that yet.

Zigzagging across the Arctic mainland in Nunavut, I had spent the preceding weeks paddling down one river, struggling up a second, then portaging for four days to get to that point: the headwaters of the Western River. In about a week, the river would spit me into Bathurst Inlet on the Arctic coast, where I had arranged to catch a floatplane back to Yellowknife. It was not the first summer I had spent on the tundra, but it was the first time I had gone alone.

The big advantage of solo travel is the ability to indulge in every whim, to follow one's nose and to explore anything that catches one's fancy. On some days this meant climbing up eskers, or following caribou trails across the flower-dappled landscape. At other times I sat in the canoe, drifting with the current while plucking my ukulele, or setting off on foot to sneak up on a herd of muskoxen, the wind whipping their shaggy coats around their ankles.

A few days before, I had paddled into an ice-choked bay and discovered pans of rotten ice that tinkled like a music box in my wake. On the shoreline I had spotted grizzly tracks in the mud and caribou scat distributed across clusters of mountain avens. Grabbing my camera bag, I had hiked out through fragrant clusters of Arctic lupines, taking pictures until the sun faded sometime after midnight.

Earlier that morning, I would have thought it was raining if I hadn't known better. Warm and snug inside my tent, I imagined that the pattering on my tent fly was incredibly peaceful. But this was not the sound of rain. It was the sound of blackflies pinging off the nylon, looking for a way to get inside. If not for the pressure in my bladder, I never would have ventured out.

But out I had to go. Cocooned in my bug shirt, I had leapt from the tent and briskly started walking while simultaneously trying to relieve myself. The trick in such a scenario is to keep moving to reduce insect attacks on the exposed parts, while at the same time not peeing on oneself. This tactic was effective on both counts. Well, mostly.

After zipping up, I had stood for a moment encapsulated within the buzzing cloud of insects, morbidly fascinated by their staggering numbers. Even if escape had meant paddling into a stiff headwind, I would have preferred that any day over dealing with the insect scourge.

It struck me then that everything was ravenous out there. The bugs with their thirst for blood; the wolves I'd seen snapping at molting geese; the lake trout that smacked my lures like a heavyweight's right hook. And me. After a long day on the river, I was always ravenous.

There was nothing like a calorie deficit to make eating monopolize your thoughts and turn food into taste-bud crack. And there was nothing like weeks of paddling, portaging, and hiking with strict rations to create those conditions by deepening ones appetite and burning through one's body fat reserves.

To take my mind off food for a while, I had tried musing about other things, like why this place—specifically the northern Arctic tundra—was so irresistible to me. I decided it has something to do with combining the exhilaration of paddling rapids, or encountering herds of migrating caribou, with the sweetness of those bug-free moments. Sitting and contemplating life beside a gurgling river is the very stuff that makes life palatable.

Much later, out on the river, I was contemplating all of this again. I reached for the cornbread. The taste washed over me, a sucker punch of flavor that merged all thoughts into one: it was worth it—the bugs, the portages, and the blisters—if only for that!

The wolverine jolted me from my cornbread-induced reverie. Appearing just a hundred and fifty meters downstream, it was the first wolverine I had ever seen in more than five thousand kilometers of northern canoe trips. Of all things wild and toothy, people know this about wolverines: they live fiercely. Powerful, tireless, and cagey—and known to successfully challenge grizzly bears for dibs on an overripe meal—wolverines are the very embodiment of wildness.

Gripping my binoculars, I saw its trademark see-sawing gait as it loped up the shoreline, its coarse brown fur rippling on its back, needles of light flashing off the streaks of blonde hair. With its head down, sniffing as it moved, the wolverine stabbed its jaws at something on the ground, gulping it down before it continued moving toward me.

With my attention riveted on the wolverine, I didn't notice the faint thumping sound coming from somewhere behind me. But when it crested the river valley, the sound of the low-flying helicopter filled my ears with an explosive roar, its whirling blades chopping the air and shredding the silence.

And so ended my moment with the only wolverine I will likely ever see.

For a month I had seen nobody. The only sounds were the wind, water, and birdsong. But somehow, in a vast area of more than a million square kilometers of wilderness, a canoeist, a wolverine, and a helicopter intersect simultaneously in a baffling and infuriating coincidence.

Whirling on its hind legs, the wolverine bolted, its sharp claws tearing into the tundra as it bounded in the only sensible direction a threatened wolverine can go: north.

For where else but the North can a wolverine find the space to express its wild nature? And where else but the North can a person tap into that vestigial wildness we all harbor inside: that primal hunger and physicality that calms the mind, enlivens our spirit and heightens our senses to the point that one can achieve nirvana by simply eating cornbread?

Nowhere but North.

Tim Irvin is a biologist, wildlife guide and photographer. He has eaten cornbread and chased wild toothy creatures across three territories and eight provinces. He is also the author of Arctic Inspired: A Tribute to the Tundra, *a book of stories and images inspired by self-propelled travels in the Arctic. You can find more of his work at www.timirvin.com.*

Yoga Matt

Yogic composure can be overrated.

By Kelly Kittel

We walked to the early morning yoga class feeling silly, like schoolgirls. But who could blame us? We were at San Marcos in Guatemala for a weeklong writing conference, and we were feeling giddy with excitement.

As we passed a stranger on the dirt path, my friend Linda tried to greet him. "Buenos dias," she said.

"Are you from Chicago?" he replied immediately. We started giggling anew, thinking this a commentary on her bad Spanish accent.

"I saw it on your T-shirt," he explained.

We realized the blue letters on her T-shirt did indeed spell CHICAGO, and for some reason we laughed even harder.

Trying to regain our yogic composure, we entered the palapa. Our instructor, Matt, and several yoginis were already folded into lotus positions with their eyes closed. They were in the process of centering themselves. All were silent. As quietly as possible, we wrestled woven-leaf mats from a stack in the corner (they were heavier than they appeared), and found our places in the circle of six. I sat directly across from Matt.

Removing my dirty hiking boots and socks, I attempted to settle in, quiet my mind, and bring myself into the present. But my runny nose wasn't cooperating. I glanced down and saw that the front corner of my yoga mat was covered in green mildew. I am allergic to mildew, which would explain the runny nose. I considered my options. I finally decided to get up and tiptoe over to my backpack, hoping that I would find a tissue in one of the compartments. No such luck. I turned around again. Matt was still silent. All eyes were closed. Nobody was watching me.

Sniffing, I crept back through the entrance in search of some tissue. But there was nothing except the piles of our unread manuscripts, stacked neatly on the bar, awaiting critiques from the participants of the writing retreat. I resigned myself to a bathroom hike. Stepping onto the trail, I realized that I had forgotten my shoes and that the pathway was dirty and damp. I tiptoed to the toilet so as to expose as little mud as possible to my feet.

On the way to the bathroom, I spotted a pile of kitchen napkins. I took a stack, then reversed my ballerina steps back to the palapa. Matt was still sitting in his perfect lotus. Everyone was silent. I quietly selected a new mat and reclaimed my place in the circle, nudging my mildewed mat aside and lowering this fresh one in its place. I was trying very hard to be inconspicuous. It seemed to be working. Finally, I crossed my legs into the lotus position, settled the napkins next to my Nalgene bottle, and began to focus on the task at hand.

As I turned my gaze inward, my eyelids began to sink. But just as they were about to shut, I saw a large cockroach crawl from underneath my new mat. My eyes snapped open. Not daring to make another sound, I watched in horror as the large insect scurried away from me. This was good, I thought. But as I watched, the insect headed straight toward Matt.

Matt was still in his perfect yogic trance. I didn't dare say a word to interrupt his meditation—hadn't I been disruptive enough already? I glanced around the circle to see if anybody else had noticed the cockroach, but they were all focused on their inner selves.

The roach reached the edge of Matt's yoga mat. I didn't know what to do, so I simply watched. Unlike the rest of us, Matt had a nonorganic, sticky mat. While he meditated, I prayed that the roach—which had briefly paused—would simply crawl beneath the inviting space of the mat's curled-up front edge. Don't roaches like the dark? Apparently not. I watched, horrified, as the roach confidently chose enlightenment over darkness, and strode purposefully toward Matt's naked toes, which were sticking out from beneath his folded knee.

The cockroach reached a point on the mat just beside my instructor's toes. It turned and proceeded to crawl parallel to Matt's foot in the direction of his ankle. If Matt was aware of the roach, his face did not show it. He was good. He was a professional. Unlike me, Matt was not distracted by a crawling insect.

Then the roach mounted Matt's bare foot and disappeared right up into the loose leg of his striped pants.

Matt's eyes snapped open. His eyes locked onto mine as he caught me staring at him.

I was about to open my mouth to speak—though I have no idea what I would have said—when Matt beat me to it. He announced that we should change to Lion Pose. This was one of my least-favorite poses. I kept my mouth shut and watched while Matt demonstrated the pose, opening his eyes and mouth impossibly wide, tilting his head back, then sticking his tongue *way* out. While shaking his head back and forth, he let out a noise that was part roar and part gargle.

My eyes were still fixed on Matt, but not for the reason he might think. Where the heck was that cockroach? Where did it go?

Matt encouraged the rest of us to join him in Lion Pose. I was not convincing. Though I tried, the puritan in me would not allow my tongue to hang out of my mouth like a panting dog. And opening my mouth wide reminded me of childhood strep-throat exams, which had always made me gag. Besides, I still wanted to know where that cockroach was hiding.

I had chosen yoga that morning to give my arms a rest after spending several days swimming in a lake the Mayans call "The Belly Button of the Planet." So one can imagine my dismay when Matt announced that we would focus on our arms. He instructed us to hold them straight out from our sides, making minor adjustments to our hands and wrists. My biceps and triceps began to scream. Eventually I couldn't take the strain, so I dropped my arms and stretched. Matt gave us a lecture on why holding the pose would build strength. I was more interested in having him stand up so I could see if that cockroach would fall out of his pantleg.

Finally, Matt changed poses—but only to a kneeling position.

Just then, we were interrupted by another member of our writing group. He had unwittingly been trailed by three local dogs, who joined in our practice with an admirable burst of enthusiasm. A blue-eyed husky bounded over and started to lick me. Nevertheless, I tried to hold my pose so that I could build strength and so that Matt wouldn't think I was weak. But the dog continued to slobber all over me.

"Ignore the dogs," said Matt.

I obeyed, pretending that I could tune out the critters—even ones that were drooling on me—like a real yogini. I was definitely in the moment.

Finally, I was rewarded for my patience. Matt stood up. I concentrated with my entire being, shifting my gaze back and forth between his face and his feet, but I detected neither a change in his composure nor a mangled insect. Where the heck did that bug go?

We followed Matt through several sun salutations before ending in Child's Pose. As my nose neared the ground in supplication, I realized that my mat was crawling with tiny insects, and wondered if the roach had left behind some of his family. I did not want my head anywhere near that bug-infested mat. While the others rested their foreheads organically, I cradled my chin in my hands and watched the activity instead. When Matt came around to correct our postures, I sat up and stretched. We both knew that I was a lost cause.

But Matt wasn't quite finished. He decided to demonstrate one final sun salutation for us, one final attempt at inspiration that I felt was directed toward me. Turning his mat sideways so that we had a better view, he executed a perfect sun salutation. I have never seen anything like it. It felt like I was watching a video or reading a yoga manual. He finished and asked if we had any questions. I wanted to ask him about the roach, but I maintained my yogic silence.

The school children began their daily drum-banging exercises across the street. Matt informed us that we should lie down in Shavasana—Corpse Pose—to complete our practice, and then he stretched out on his own sticky mat. All was right in his world.

I was getting hungry. The drums were loud and distracting, and I couldn't maintain the pretense of continuing my long-abandoned practice. As I got up and left the palapa, Matt lay on his mat in perfect, serene repose.

I never saw that cockroach again.

Kelly Kittel and her family live in a yurt on the coast of Oregon, where they share space with a resident herd of elk, none of which practice yoga (as far as she knows). She was recently published in Getting Out: Your Guide to Leaving America, *and is currently writing a travel memoir about living in Costa Rica. Kelly also writes a blog,* Where in the World are the Kittels? *which can be visited at http://www.kittelposse.blogspot.ca/*

Tarzan

He is one stubborn little tree swinger.

By Natasha Deen

A few years ago, when GPS technology was still new and OnStar wasn't standard-issue in GM vehicles, my husband came home and said he wanted to buy a portable GPS device.

My spousal radar started beeping and a voice inside my head said, *You're going to regret this. Don't let him do it.*

It seemed like an odd request. You see, my husband is one of those guys who could navigate through an action scene in a Bruce Willis movie. He gets us to where we need to go even with the sketchiest of directions. On the flip side, I'm still not sure what a township road is. Of the two of us, it should have been me agitating for the device.

Something's going on, said my inner voice. *It's time to start asking some hard questions.*

Of course, although men and women use the same words, we speak completely different languages. The proof of this can be found in any home where a husband asks, "Are you ready?" and the wife immediately replies, "Yes, I'll be done in a minute." It's astounding how much divergence of opinion there is on what constitutes "a minute."

Thus, I should not have been surprised by our roundabout conversation.

"Are you sure we should buy this?" *Are you kidding me? You can find your way out of the Bermuda Triangle! What's really going on here?*

"Yeah, I think I need it for work." *Unbeknownst to you, I've managed to scoop you and acquire the news on the latest cool gadget.*

"Work?" *What? How dare you scoop me on the latest cool gadget!*

"Yeah, Mike has one and it really comes in handy." *Oh, come on. Commme onnn. Mike has one. I want one.*

"Really? Mike has one?" *Oh, I get it. Your brother has one and now you want to have one, too.*

"It'll be helpful when we're traveling out of town, too. And it has great graphics." *Baby, it's both bright and shiny.*

He had seduced me. We went to the store and purchased the GPS, which I immediately nicknamed Tarzan.

We brought home our little digital baby and opened the manual. The first thing we had to do—according to the instructions—was to loosen the screws on the main piece so that the base and suction cup could be attached. Then we had to reattach everything. This sounded a bit odd, so I double-checked the manual to make sure that I'd gotten the instructions right.

Now, I use the term "manual" loosely here, as it clearly wasn't a manual in the purest sense of the word. It would have been more accurate to describe it as a packet of sheets that required an engineering degree to understand, coupled with a great deal of faith, determination, and an ability to decipher complex hieroglyphics while cursing loudly and wishing you'd drunk a bottle of scotch before attempting the "installation."

Nevertheless, the so-called manual instructed me to loosen the screws. So I did. As I was finishing, the spring under the screw sprang from my grasp and ricocheted off a nearby wall, landing with a *ping!* in some unknown location in the living room.

I looked up. My husband was watching me with That Look. You probably know the one, ladies: the why-are-women-so-silly look. Some might also know this as the thank-God-I'm-a-man-and-don't-do-boneheaded-things-like-that look.

Since I'm more than a woman, but also a lady, I refrained from pointing out that on the scoreboard of Boneheaded Moves, my husband was still winning the game. Instead, I smiled sweetly and said, "Whoops."

We stopped the installation to go hunting for the spring, which took us a good fifteen minutes to find. At that point, my husband—the light of my life—looked at the fragmented Tarzan and said in that macho way that all of us ladies adore: "Here, let me try." He reached over and took the GPS device out of my hand.

My husband and I have been together a long time, and I know better than to argue now. This is mostly because history has taught me (and every woman in existence) that Karma is a girl, and when a boy uses That Tone, he's usually going to get a kick in the butt.

I decided that I needed a break, so I went into my study.

In the end, Lady Karma didn't kick my husband in the butt;

that's because she decided to poke him in the eye instead. As he was trying to complete Step One and loosen the second screw, the spring popped off and shot between his cheek and the rim of his glasses, where it hit him directly in the eyeball. I'm not lying.

All I can say is that I'm very happy I learned about this *after the fact*, because if I'd been in the living room at that moment I would have started laughing and would probably be signing my divorce papers right now instead of documenting this incident.

Defeated, my husband called me back.

Working as a team we finally, *finally*, managed to assemble the device and turn it on. Nothing. I reread the instructions, but there was nothing to suggest that we'd done something wrong.

I logged on to my computer and navigated to the company's web site. Unbelievably, there was no Contact Us button, no contact form, and no phone number. The menus were arranged in such a way as to make me feel like I had entered a convenience store that was a front for money laundering. At this point, I began to suspect that the GPS was a piece of crap, and that the reason there wasn't an 800 number is because the company also knew it was a piece of crap and didn't want to be reminded.

I went back to my husband and said, "Let's take it outside and see what happens."

Well, miracle of miracles, the GPS started to work. It began processing, and within a few short minutes it had successfully determined our exact global position. My husband was so pleased that I didn't have the heart to mention that a GPS that doesn't work inside is not very useful. (I also envisioned the police pulling him over to ask why he was hanging out of the driver's-side window with a GPS device in his hand.) But I tried to cut the little Neanderthal some slack. After all, there aren't many roofs in the jungle.

We went back inside, where I waited for my husband to realize something I already knew: the software would have to be updated. I was curious to see how he would react. My guy's an amazing man, but asking him to do anything with technology is like asking Tarzan to tango: they could probably do it, but it's cruel to ask and you wouldn't want to watch. Bottom line: I knew that *I* would be the one who would have to update *his* toy. He brought this up at bedtime when I was too tired to fight off his flattery, and I heard myself agree to update Tarzan's software every six months.

The next day, we were excited to try out the GPS. I hadn't had time to update the software yet, but I didn't see a problem. It wasn't like we were going to a new part of Edmonton. We climbed into the car, turned on the GPS, and heard something like, "Me Tarzan. Me GPS device. Me show you where to go." Tarzan had a surprisingly feminine voice, but who was I to judge?

While I can't recall the exact words we exchanged with Tarzan over the course of our drive, let me try to paint a picture of what this experience *felt* like.

"Hello Tarzan, this is where we want to go," I said. I punched in the address.

"Me no find that."

Hmmm … better try that again.

"Me no find that."

After the fifth attempt at entering the address, I was starting to lose my patience.

"Now Tarzan, you know perfectly well the address exists. It's an *old* town and an *old* address. It's in your database. Be a good little Neanderthal and show me."

"No. Me no find. It no exist." And with that, Tarzan flopped down most unceremoniously. Thankfully, the "loincloth" covered all his cords and USB ports.

"Tarzan, here's the address. Direct me." I tried entering it again.

"No. Me no find. You want to go to West End? I take you to Mall."

At that point, my husband had to wrestle the hammer out of my hand. "Maybe the maps need to be updated," he said. "Let's see if Tarzan can find the town."

So I entered the name of the town without an address. Mercifully, Tarzan said that he knew where it was. My husband put the car in gear and we pulled out of the cul-de-sac.

Conversation with Tarzan continued as we drove. "Right turn in six hundred meters … right turn in five hundred meters … right turn in four hundred meters … right turn in three hundred meters…"

I wanted to point out that I wasn't blind and that, in fact, I was able to see the right turn from *before* six hundred meters. But I refrained, mainly because he was cooperating in that aren't-I-the-smartest-kid-in-the-class-with-hand-waving-in-the-air kind of way, and I wanted to give him some positive reinforcement.

Tarzan continued counting down the meters at every turn. After thirty minutes on the road, I made my husband pull over at the liquor store. Since we weren't allowed to have open liquor in the car, I lashed myself to the roof and drank until I couldn't hear, "Left turn in six hundred meters … left turn in five hundred meters … left turn in four hundred meters…"

The drive went … well, it went. When Tarzan tried—on numerous occasions—to drown us by insisting that we should execute a left-hand turn that would have landed us in a lake, I wondered if we'd accidentally gotten Psycho Tarzan. When we inevitably ignored him and drove past, he would then implore us to complete a U-turn and make a right turn … into the same lake.

When we got home, I decided to update the software because I realized my husband was really attached to this thing and I wanted him to be happy. So, like any good idiot who hasn't learned her lesson, I went and updated the GPS.

Well, I tried to. But Tarzan proved to be a stubborn little tree swinger.

The GPS wouldn't recognize the memory stick. My computer wouldn't recognize the GPS. I felt like the mediator between two bickering children who were standing at opposite ends of a room with their backs turned and arms crossed. Plans A and B were shot. I went back to the company's web site and discovered that if I registered the product, they would e-mail me an 800 number. I tried not to think about the possible reasons for a company having a secret toll-free number, and did as I was told.

Ten minutes later I had a number.

I called and was immediately put on hold. An hour later, an agent finally came on the line. Fortunately, it only took her five minutes to provide me with an assessment of our problem: "Take it back. It sounds like the software is corrupted."

Corrupted. Just like my will to live.

We went to the store and returned the product. On the way out, I decided that I should try to make my husband feel better, so I bought him a map.

"It doesn't have an LCD display or take voice commands," I said as I handed it to him. "But it'll work. Even under a roof."

Natasha Deen may have been the first woman to ever get lost while walking in a straight line. Despite her lack of directional sense, she is a capable write for both adults and children. Her most recent book is titled True Grime. *You can visit her at www.natashadeen.com or follow her on Twitter and Facebook.*

Snooper

The life and times of an accidental secret agent.

By Sterling Haynes

When I purchased my Senso hearing aids, they opened up a whole new world to me. I suddenly found myself in a new digital age of eavesdropping. The acoustic abilities made me into a mole. I sometimes envisioned myself as an undercover agent, though I doubt the FBI, CIA, CSIS, or the KGB would hire a deaf old man as a snooper.

My new BTE (Behind The Ear) aids were comparable to a very powerful computer. The glossy brochure informed me that their processors "sampled sound signals a million times every second," adjusting sound automatically and turning those signals into smooth, mellifluous voices. I believe my Sensos did what the brochure promised and more. Not only did they suppress noise and enhance speech, but under certain conditions, my hearing aids brought me a wealth of unexpected information.

Whenever I would drive across the floating bridge in Kelowna, British Columbia—or fly in an aircraft—my freeway became an information highway.

I understand that this effect had to do with being surrounded by metal. As my audiologist explained to me, transmissions from cell phones, and from the radios in the cockpits of airplanes, were transferred to my hearing aids by "the electromagnetic conduction effect of the metal superstructures." Whenever traffic was delayed on the bridge or on the runway, aircrew or drivers with cell phones would start talking, and I became a reluctant spy. When I traveled the highways and skyways, I was perpetually bombarded with snippets of conversation that were happy, angry, or erotic—I never knew which to expect.

About once every week, if conditions were optimal on the bridge, I caught pieces of conversation that were related to business deals, marital spats, or the kids' shenanigans at home. Once I even heard about a sexual tryst slated for the afternoon. Unfortunately, I reached the end of the bridge before I could get all the titillating details.

The most startling conversation I heard took place while I was sitting on a Houston runway. It was between the pilot, the flight engineer, and a stewardess in the cockpit. The conversation started like this, with the pilot speaking to the flight engineer:

Pilot: "When are you going to get that rudder fixed? It's been malfunctioning for over a month. You call yourself a flight engineer, but nothing ever gets fixed around here. We're going to have a serious problem if you don't get off your butt. If you guys don't stay focused and keep your eyes and ears open, there could be serious consequences. Even a catastrophe."

Engineer: "Yeah, Yeah. You guys are always complaining. Sitting here in your air-conditioned cockpit while I'm sweating it out on the tarmac. The rudder will hold up for this flight.

When you get back, we'll take this aircraft out of service. Better fill in another report."

Then I saw the engineer leave by way of the front door.

A new conversation began between the pilot and one of the stewardesses. "Hi ya'll, boys. That was quite a party last night at the hotel. Ah hate the layover here. Ah'll be glad to get to Belize City. Ah love the beaches. Ah'll try on my new bikini. Ya boys are gonna love it. That Cuban rum is overproof, ya know. Hope ya ole headache gets well."

After this conversation, I saw a gorgeous flight attendant come out the cockpit door and start to prepare hot breakfasts. When she brought me the breakfast tray after takeoff, I said, "That was some party you and the crew had last night at the hotel. You must have great recuperative powers. Thanks for the breakfast."

She turned a deep crimson and quickly left. I caught her eyes a few times during the flight; she blushed, but didn't take the tray away. Upon deplaning, she never did tell me to have a good day.

Three weeks later, on the return flight to Houston from Belize City, we boarded the same Boeing 737. I had an opportunity to ask the copilot if the rudder had been fixed and was in good working condition.

The copilot gave me a quizzical look and said, "Yes, it has been fixed. How did you know about it?"

I fumbled with my hearing aids and replied, "What was that you said? My batteries just stopped working."

He looked at me and then left for the safety of his cockpit.

So the moral of my story is this: If you have hearing aids, keep them plugged into your ears at all times. Don't leave home without 'em. You never know, Scotland Yard or *The National Enquirer* might be interested.

Sterling Haynes has taken to writing humorous stories in his retirement. His tales have appeared in many magazines, journals and newspapers and often have a medical theme. Sterling's first book was titled Bloody Practice *(Caitlin Press), and was on the BC bestseller list for two months. His latest book,* Wake Up Call: Tales from a Frontier Doctor, *is now available as an e-book through Indigo's Kobo and Barnes & Noble's Nook.*

Lake Expectations

Wanted: cooperative animals that enjoy posing for pictures.

By Philip Torrens

L ooking back, I definitely oversold the wildlife viewing. I'd done the Bowron Lakes canoe route solo before, and had immensely enjoyed this lovely circuit of mountain lakes linked by rivers and portages. On that trip, I'd spent at least an hour sitting in my sea kayak one afternoon, taking photo after photo as a moose placidly chewed his waterweed salad just a few boat lengths away.

While convincing my wife Leanne and our friend Heidi to come with me on a repeat of the trip, I'd gushed endlessly about that particular experience. By the time I'd finished the sales pitch, they were convinced that the Bowron canoe circuit would be the Disney Jungle Cruise park ride, Canadian Edition. Every bend in every river would reveal exotic animals, primping cooperatively for pictures as we drifted by. They could hardly wait.

The Bowron Lakes Canoe Circuit is located in central British Columbia, and is a well-traveled route during the summer months. Because of its popularity, there is a mandatory pre-trip orientation at the ranger's cabin, which includes watching a video with advice on avoiding trouble with bears. Apparently, though, the film was produced on a budget of seven dollars and forty-two cents, as it consists of a mix of stock footage and painfully staged scenes of bear encounters. It puts the camp in camping, one might say. If Ed Wood had made a horror movie in the "teenagers in the woods" genre, this would be it. The film's takeaways boil down to: One, store your food in the bear-proof lockers provided at each campsite. And two, don't smear yourself with peanut butter before going to bed.

The first five days of our trip went well. Although most people who paddle the Bowron Lakes use canoes, the portage trails are wide enough that one can use a set of portable wheels to portage other types of boats—such as our double and single kayaks—from one lake to the next. Thanks to my brilliant planning, on three of the first four nights we had slept in one of several cabins that are available at select points along the circuit. On the one night we'd been forced to sleep in our tents, we'd had only intermittent rain showers. The weather was biding its time, lulling us into a false sense of security.

We'd also seen some wildlife: A woodpecker. A hummingbird. A toad. Several mice that had scampered across our heads as we slept in the cabins. Untold millions of mosquitoes. A pair of moose in the distance. Very nice, but also very small. Size clearly matters to the womenfolk. Where were the big beasts? When were we going to get up close and personal with nature?

We did hear a bear banging against the food lockers late one night, but thankfully, that was when we were safely in a cabin. Curiously, nobody showed any inclination to go wildlife viewing by headlamp.

It was on the fifth day that things got a bit challenging. After an exhilarating run down a river, we'd battled headwinds on two large lakes—Lanezi and Sandy. We'd had to pull off the water to wait out one particularly severe squall. By the time we landed at that evening's campsite, two of our party were tired and a bit grumpy. (Hint: neither one was me.)

We were in our tents again that night when we heard the onset of some sprinkles. That is, if you want to classify what sounded like blasts from multiple fire hoses as "sprinkles."

Keen to save weight on the portages, Heidi had talked me into lending her a prototype ultralight tent that I was field-testing. The manufacturer had trimmed a lot of grams off this model by dispensing with superfluous features, which included the ability to stay dry on the inside while it was raining. It wasn't clear whether the fly fabric was actually leaking, or whether it was interior condensation that was sieving through the interior mesh canopy. Regardless, the result was the same: Heidi's down sleeping bag had blotted into paper mache. By the next morning, she was one cold, tired, and unhappy camper, her normally sweet temperament now bordering on the sullen.

On the bright side, it was no longer pouring. It had dawned into what the Irish call a "soft" day, with only the occasional drifting shower and a wee bit of chill in the air. I'd made myself a cup of coffee. As I leaned back in my folding chair, dry beneath the kitchen tarp with a hot, creamy, sweet brew warming my hands and insides, I looked out over the mist-shrouded lake. A pair of loons glided on the silver surface, occasionally bouncing their distinctive cries off the trees on the far shore. Ah, the quintessential Canadian wilderness experience.

It just doesn't get any better than this, I thought to myself.

As if on cue, Leanne tromped into view en route to the outhouse, swaddled like a street person in her unzipped sleeping bag. As she passed, she muttered loudly, "Anyone who likes this crap is outta their freaking mind."

Let it never be said that I'm a stereotypical guy, insensitive to the subtle signals that women send. I hastily consulted the map. By skipping a side trip to see Cariboo Falls, we could complete the circuit and be out of the woods in one or two more sleeps, rather than three. Would the ladies like that? They most certainly would. The rotten weather they could cope with. But combined with the lack of sexy wildlife, it was simply too much to take.

The prospect of hotel rooms and hot showers energized the women. They paddled like Olympic rowers on crack. By midafternoon we had crossed Sandy Lake, paddled a section of river, lined down a creek, made a major portage, and paddled another midsized body of water (Babcock Lake, for those following along on your maps at home).

We'd decided to have a late lunch at the landing point on Babcock's western shore before completing the short portage to little Skoi Lake. In preparation, we'd already strapped the kayaks onto their folding carts and transferred some cargo into the cockpits to balance the weight over the wheels.

We enjoyed our picnic on the north side of Babcock, sitting beside one of the rangers' boats. Park staffers are the only ones who are allowed to use powerboats in the Bowron Lakes. Being lazy sorts, they're loath to singlehandedly portage an aluminum runabout complete with outboard motor between every body of water, so they keep a separate boat on each lake. This one sat on its wooden launch ramp on the other side of the lakeside beach.

It was while we were cleaning up after lunch that Leanne noticed a trio of creatures galloping along the lake's northern beach. They were a fair distance away, but closing quickly as they followed the curve of the lakeshore toward us. Plumes of spray sparkled in the sun as they wove in and out of the shallows.

Wildlife at last! Well, it was about time. This was more like it. What was the big beast in the lead? A cow moose. And behind her? Her calf. And behind the calf? Another calf? No, wait, let them get closer. It's a … a … a mother grizzly!

We held a very quick conference. Manning the kayaks was out—it would have taken too long to untie them and get them onto the water. Running seemed certain to provoke the bear's hunting response. Standing our ground seemed the only option. We quickly bunched together on the far side of the rangers' boat and drew our canisters of bear spray out of their holsters. It felt like the equivalent of whipping out a water gun to stop a charging rhino.

In the lead, Mother Moose was the first to spot the rangers' boat lying across her path. Her body masked it from the bear. At the last possible second, Mother Moose cranked a hard left into the woods, with her baby following close on her tail. Caught by surprise, and unable to corner as sharply, Ma Grizz fetched up against the boat's far side with an impressive *bang!*

A moment later, her front paws appeared one by one on the boat's far gunwale. As she started to haul herself up on her hind legs, head shaking from side to side, it was hard not to laugh: the stunned cartoon critter recovering from a self-inflicted headshot. Then she reached her full, awesome height. The giggles died in our throats. She seemed to tower several feet above us, and each paw looked larger than a human head.

She was obviously aware of us, as she began blinking myopically and sniffing the air, trying to puzzle out what manner of creatures we were. That was our cue, as advised in every wilderness survival book, to try to look and sound as big and intimidating as possible. *We're a bunch of badasses*, the message is supposed to be. *Don't mess with us or we'll bust a crap in our pants.*

It was a pretty unconvincing performance. What were intended to be baritone roars of "Go away bear!" came out as falsetto squeaks. Picture a trio of Richard Simmons look-alikes trying to play Rambo and you've got the general idea.

I swear I saw the bear raise a skeptical eyebrow. *Are you talking to me? You've got to be kidding.* One could almost hear her thinking, *Well, I was going to bring moose takeout home for the kids. But these soft pink things might hit the spot. And there will be one for each of us.*

Fortunately for us, at the critical moment of decision, the cracks of breaking underbrush came from the direction where the moose were making their getaway. The sound seemed to snap Ma Grizz out of her reverie and remind her of her original dinner plans. With an explosive snort, she dropped onto all fours and charged after her prey.

Slowly, tentatively, and with a great deal of relief, we lowered our spray canisters and unbundled from one another. During the debrief, we realized that we'd been very fortunate indeed: if Ma Grizz had brought down one of the moose on the far side of the boat, and then discovered us, she'd have assumed we were rivals for her kill. That could have ended poorly.

Privately, we hoped our unwitting diversion had bought Mother Moose and her calf enough time to make their getaway. We wanted to believe the moose were returning the favor, luring Ma Grizz far enough away that she wouldn't be inclined to backtrack and claim us as consolation prizes. But we had no way to be sure. So, amped up on a potent cocktail of adrenaline and apprehension, we resumed the portage to Skoi Lake.

Heidi and I pulled the boats on their wheels. Leanne stalked along the trail with half of a kayak paddle gripped fiercely across her chest, eyes darting from side to side, trying to peer into the deep, dark woods. She looked like a Viking clutching a two-handed battle-ax, on full alert for ambush. I smiled indulgently. I'd chosen those paddles specifically for their ultralight construction. Clearly, they wouldn't pack much of a wallop.

"Well, girls," I observed jovially as I wheeled the double kayak past Leanne, "I trust that was enough wildlife for you." It turns out that even with the blade turned flat, a featherweight paddle delivers an impressive blow to the back of the head.

Philip Torrens has been exploring the Canadian wilderness for decades. He started out as a hiker, but has also tried ski touring and snowshoeing. These days, most of his backcountry travel is by kayak or canoe. The incident in this story was not his first close encounter of the furry kind. You can read about one of his other misadventures in Mugged by a Moose, *where he writes about a middle-of-the-night encounter with a polar bear in Canada's Arctic.*

Hillbillies

Is that banjo music I hear?

By Sylvia Fleming

I'm a spontaneous person by nature. Life just seems so much more interesting when you force yourself out of a routine and embrace the unknown. Perhaps that's why, when my friend Patricia called me to see if I wanted to spend some time catching up at the Wheels Inn in Chatham, Ontario, I jumped at the chance. We both had a couple of weeks off, and we figured this would be a great opportunity to unwind and spend some time together.

It was early spring, so there were no holiday crowds to contend with. When Patricia arrived, I took over the driving, as she doesn't like to do it. We immediately set out on Highway 401 for Chatham. Being women, and not having had a good conversation for some time, we were lost in our chatter when we suddenly realized that we'd passed the turnoff to the Inn.

I looked at my friend, and knowing her parents were in Florida, I said, "Gee, the border isn't far from here. Are you game to keep driving?" She quickly and enthusiastically agreed to it. Without any further planning, we decided to see how far we could go before turning back.

We crossed the border at Windsor and started our journey south. We drove as far as Bowling Green, Ohio, that first night, where we checked ourselves into a hotel. When we awoke in the morning, all I knew was that an adventure awaited us and that I was excited to get going. We studied the road map and agreed to stay off the main roads; the plan was to keep driving and see where we ended up, to let spontaneity rule the day.

As we drove, we saw places and things that I didn't know existed. We traveled south into Tennessee and Kentucky and had dinner at the refurbished train station in Chattanooga. We stayed for a night in Shakertown and traveled on an old wagon trail through the Smoky Mountains. In what could only be the hollows of Kentucky, we stopped at an inn for lunch and were mistaken for horse buyers. I'm not ashamed to admit that we went along with the conversation! It was fun to pretend, and because my friend knows how to "talk horses," she was able to carry the conversation quite well.

While traveling on a winding road through one mountainous area, we noticed a little café with pretty lace curtains, so we decided to stop and have some lunch. We were in a very small town in what seemed like the middle of nowhere. Along with a few houses, there was only the café, a bank, and a garage—all named after the town. By this time we were in the habit of taking our cameras with us everywhere, so we entered the café with them strung over our shoulders. We were dressed in well-cut jeans, jackets, and high cowboy boots. I think we looked pretty good!

As we entered, it felt like we had walked through a time warp back into the 1950s. Down the right side of the restaurant were several booths, each one with its own tabletop jukebox. I know that some restaurants try to recreate a Fifties theme with this type of decor, but it wasn't hard to tell that this was the original thing. On the left side of the room was a long counter with a half-dozen red leather stools that swiveled. On those stools sat five or six men who could only be described as hillbillies—they wore high boots, wide-brimmed hats, and jeans held up with suspenders. As they heard us enter, they turned in unison and stared at us. That would have been fine, except that they didn't turn back. As we walked over to a booth and sat down, their eyes followed our every move.

My clever girlfriend picked the bench that would allow her to sit with her back to the men, which of course left me facing them. This made me nervous to say the least, and when I'm nervous, I begin to laugh. I picked up one of the large menus and began reading it, hoping to calm myself down. But when I peeked out from behind it I could see that the men were still staring, which made me laugh even harder.

I couldn't believe what I was reading on the menu, either. The prices were so low that it just proved we had stepped through a time warp. Hamburgers were one dollar; french fries and Coca Cola were fifty cents each. That sent me into another fit of muffled laughter.

A moment later, a waitress dressed in a frilly white apron came over and asked what we would like to order. At least, I think that's what she was asking. I don't know for sure because her dialect was very strong. Trying to contain myself, I told her that we needed more time to look over the menus. As she walked away, I peered out from behind the large menu again. And you know what? The men were *still* staring.

The next thing I knew, Patricia had started laughing, too. This made me feel marginally better, as I was no longer the only one in this embarrassing situation. For the next few minutes, we continued to hide behind our menus, the men continued to stare, and we continued to laugh. My friend did her best to put an end to it, but we just couldn't stop.

With no warning, my friend announced that she had to visit the restroom. I told her—quite firmly—that she couldn't leave me there alone. But she explained that she couldn't hold it any longer. So she got up, walked past the staring hillbillies, and passed through a door at the back of the restaurant. Alone, and with the menu still wrapped around my head, I sat there with tears rolling down my face. I was laughing that hard! Every time I took a glance, I could see that the men's eyes were still firmly fixed on me. It was becoming unbearable. Had these men never seen anyone from outside their tiny hamlet before?

It felt like an eternity before my friend returned. She was pale-faced and laughing so hard that tears were running down her face, too.

The men were still staring.

She sat down and whispered, "You have to go to the restroom!"

"No, I don't," I replied.

"Yes, you do," she said. "Go."

"No, I *don't*," I replied, this time more firmly.

"You *have* to. Don't question it. Please, just go."

"Oh my gosh, I can't believe you've talked me into this." I wanted to take the menu with me to hide my face, but I knew that would be rude. Grudgingly, I put the menu down, collected my wits, and opened the door she had just returned through.

After stepping through the door, I found myself in a room with boxes piled everywhere. It definitely wasn't a restroom. In the far corner I saw another door, so I proceeded toward it. Before opening it, I noticed a pipe just above the floor level that ran across the bottom of the doorway. I opened the door, stepped over the pipe, and entered another room of about the same size with more boxes piled everywhere.

Lo and behold, in the far corner was the toilet. But it stood on a platform that was facing the corner wall. I pictured my friend sitting there and trying to do her business with the entire room behind her. Laughing harder, I went back out to the restaurant. Believe it or not, the men were still staring, and Patricia was now in hysterics with the menu wrapped around her face.

My friend leaned over and explained what had happened to her. As she was sitting on the toilet in this very odd room, feeling the great expanse of the room behind her, the lights went out. She immediately pictured us being kidnapped and murdered. With her heart in her throat, she got up and carefully edged her way around the dark room, knocking over boxes as she went. She finally came to the door and threw it open. But as she ran out, she tripped over the pipe and fell flat on her face.

Well, that was enough. There was no more containing us. We agreed that we had to get out of there. We got up, picked up our belongings, and literally ran out the door. I could feel hillbilly eyes boring into my back as we departed.

Once outside, I took a picture of the café. When I look at that picture now, I can still see through the window, past the pretty lace curtains, and envision those hillbilly men sitting at the counter with their eyes fixed on us. And then I burst out laughing all over again.

Sylvia Fleming has a passion for travel. Road-tripping without an agenda is something she inadvertently discovered many years ago, and she now takes on the challenge of it whenever possible. This is her first story for a Summit Studios anthology.

Ten Thousand Cows

*Negotiating your daughter's hand in marriage,
African style.*

By Tim Tentcher

Our journey together as a family has led us down a lot of
amazing roads. And many of our favorite memories have
happened along roads less traveled.

A few years ago we flew to Africa for several weeks of wildlife
safaris and cultural interactions. Our daughter Rachel was sixteen
at the time. With blond hair, blue eyes, and a sparkling personality,
Rachel would have an effect on some of the local tribesmen that
my wife and I were not prepared for.

We hired a guide named Moses for our journey across the
Serengeti—which proved to be an excellent decision. While
the Serengeti is a dusty place during the summer dry season,
Moses showed us that there was still an abundance of life. Like any
experienced guide, he knew where to look for the most colorful
wildlife and cultural experiences.

One morning, while having tea at the edge of the Ngorongoro
Crater, we were approached by two Maasai warriors dressed in
their traditional red Shúkà, a type of sheet they wrap around their
bodies. While the Maasai have traditionally been cattle rustlers,

they have found other ways to make a shilling in the Serengeti. One of those ways is to ask tourists to pay for the privilege of taking their picture. Unfortunately, we had recently visited an entire village of photogenic Maasai warriors, so we told them we had enough photos.

That's when they noticed Rachel. They walked over to where she was sitting and started jumping up and down. This soon brought eight more young Maasai from the bushes, seemingly from out of nowhere, and soon they were all jumping excitedly while talking amongst themselves. Now, as we were to learn, jumping in the Maasai culture means that the men are aroused and very happy. Moses came down and started to interpret what they were saying. He explained that one of them was smitten with Rachel, and that he thought she was a shimmering vision of sensuality. Moses further translated that he was willing to offer one hundred cows to me in exchange for her hand in marriage. Moses saw the humor in this and, since he suspected they were joking, he started the bidding. Somehow, we got them up to ten thousand cows, as Rachel was a real prize.

Moses sent them off to get the cows while Rachel—unsure if this was a joke—ran to her mother and exclaimed that we had just sold her for ten thousand cows! I explained to my wife that it was all in good fun, but for some reason she failed to see the humor in it. She grabbed the keys for Moses's Land Rover, fired up the engine, and started driving down the road, determined to save her girl from the lovestruck Maasai. After chasing the truck on foot, I managed to stop them and promise my wife never to jest in such a way again. She grudgingly accepted my apology and let me and a somewhat startled Moses back into his vehicle.

Partway through the trip, Moses told us of a remote tribe of hunter-gatherers who were just beginning to show Westerners their lifestyle. He explained that it would be a long journey to find them, but if we were successful, it would provide us with a rare cultural experience. We were thrilled by the idea—not only because of the remoteness, but because the tribe reputedly spoke an ancient click language. I would later learn that the Hadza people, in fact, are the last full-time hunter-gatherers in all of Africa.

We traveled cross-country much of the way, and the lack of roads meant that we spent a lot of time getting lost. Moses had to stop frequently to ask the locals for directions. Eventually, we arrived at a small hut and were told that if we hired a click language guide, he would help us to find the elusive Hadza tribe.

We pitched our tent and waited. A few hours later, the guide came back to tell us that the tribe would be glad to greet us in the morning.

We woke up before dawn and embarked in our Land Rover through bush that seemed to be taking us into no man's land. After about an hour of brain-rattling cross-country travel, we stopped the vehicle and got out. We walked a short distance. Then, without fanfare, a fellow who looked like he had stepped out of the Stone Age appeared in front of us. He spoke to our guide with a series of clicks, and then our guide motioned for us to follow him.

The Hadza turned out to be Stone Age with a mix of the modern. We were told that the tribe had recently started wearing western clothes, and we could see a mixture of T-shirts and animal skin garments. There were no huts—just thick bushes where the tribe had hung animal skins to provide some rudimentary shelter. We watched as they ate a semi-cooked bone; then they lit a small pipe and started passing it to one another. The smell reminded me of the Swinging Sixties, so we asked the guide what they were doing. The guide explained that the men liked to "get happy" before hunting, and to do this they smoked pot.

They had soon finished and were ready for the hunt. They ran off into the bushes and we trotted along behind them. A few moments later, the men emerged from the bushes with a rat squirming at the business end of an arrow. That's when the hunt really began, and the men took off into the bush at such a fast pace that we thought we had lost them. But we shouldn't have worried. They found us again, emerging with a large guinea fowl in hand. The hunters proceeded to make a fire and cleaned the bird right in front of us—no water required! The bird was soon roasting on the fire, and not long after, it was ready to eat. The men ate the bird in a matter of minutes, smacking their lips and licking their fingers as though it had been prepared by Colonel Sanders himself.

After the meal, the hunters' eyes were on dessert. I noticed that one of them was staring at Rachel with a lovesick gaze. He spoke to our guide, and the guide translated his offer: the hunter confessed that our daughter had stolen his heart, and that he was prepared to give us four baboons for her hand in marriage. I chuckled at the absurdity of the situation, but the hunter shook his spear at me and told me not to make fun of him. He upped his ante, telling us through the translator that he would offer us six baboons. He assured us that the Germans he had met a few weeks earlier loved baboon!

I stopped chuckling. In a serious tone, I tried to explain that we were a vegetarian tribe, but thanked him for his gracious offer. The guide then translated that he would sweeten the deal by offering four gallons of honey in addition to the six baboons. We again thanked him for the kind offer and said no. He looked downtrodden, but eventually the awkward situation ended. We all got up and walked back to their camp.

For her part, Rachel later admitted that the hunter had an attractive and muscular body. The fact that he lived in the bush was a real turn-off, though!

Traveling with a blond teenager in Africa has its stresses, but it certainly added to our catalog of stories. I had always been more concerned about the boys in Canada. Little did we know how many suitors we would find for her in the heart of the Serengeti.

Tim Tentcher and his family have traveled extensively in pursuit of the world's most scrumptious vegetarian recipes. A self-professed foodie, Tentcher recently released What a Wonderful World!—*a cookbook that shares the best ethnic recipes that his family has come across. You can visit him online at www.crossingculturescuisine. com.*

Adventures in Moving

Or how I became acquainted with Murphy's Law.

By Alice Newton

At our Canadian bed-and-breakfast, we proudly proclaim, "We Promise Our Guests the Sun, Moon and Stars—and We Deliver!" U-Haul promises, "Adventures in Moving." Well, I'm here to tell you that we're not the only ones who make good on our promises!

The reason for our move was to bring half of our worldly belongings from British Columbia, where we operate our bed-and-breakfast during the summer months, to a newly acquired five-acre "ranchette" in Florida, where we planned to spend our winters.

We had a lot to move. Between us, we had acquired detritus from two previous marriages, plus two households' worth of paraphernalia from my husband Jack's late relatives. It had been our intention to share these goodies with his kids. Unfortunately, one had chosen to live in a furnished apartment with no storage facilities in Victoria, while the other had moved to Pittsburgh and already amassed more crocheted doilies than the Queen Mother. There was nothing to do but divide the payload between our two homes.

We were dismayed to learn that renting the cheapest one-way U-Haul vehicle and driving it from Canada's West Coast to the Gulf of Mexico would set us back more than five thousand dollars—not to mention fuel, insurance, and other expenses. After much deliberating, we decided to buy our own trailer.

We were thrilled to learn of an old mobile observatory that had been pushing up daisies in a farmer's field for several years. The trailer had been built to tow our astronomy club's telescope around to "star parties," but was seldom used anymore. Moreover, it featured the rather attractive price tag of one dollar. So we bought it and had the unit's faulty brakes repaired, the telescope pier removed, and the rolling roof welded shut. Getting the trailer from field to freeway put a modest nine-hundred-dollar dent in our relocation budget.

We were starting to feel downright giddy about all the money we had saved until we realized that our sports car did not have the towing capacity to drag the beast south. Saddened, Jack traded in his slick Fiero for an old Chevy Suburban, which had a great tow package and enough mustard to pass everything with ease (except the gas pumps).

We made a safe journey to Florida, retired the trailer to the backyard for use as a garden shed, and drove the Suburban extensively, since gas at the time was under a dollar per gallon.

That would not be the end of the line, however. Four years later, while visiting Tucson, Arizona for a solar conference, we fell head-over-heels in love with the desert. All it took was a romantic evening in a courtyard lit with *luminaria* lanterns and surrounded by giant saguaro cacti, where we were serenaded by melodic mariachis. Florida's gopher tortoises and armadillos were no match for the enchanting desert skies or the thrilling yips of coyotes. When we returned to Florida, we placed a two-minute phone call and sold our home. We were moving to Arizona!

In preparation for its decommissioning as a storage shed, we outfitted the old trailer with new tires and gave it a sparkling white paint job. We did nothing to the Suburban, however, which by this time was suffering metal fatigue and shedding body parts at regular intervals. We looked like the Beverly Hillbillies. If we turned on the turn signal, the cruise control went off. Whenever we lowered the tailgate window, it fell out. The brake pedal was secured with a bungee cord. We hung a sign on the Suburban that said, "Go Ahead and Make My Day—Steal My Car!" But nobody seemed to want it. So we decided that it would live out its remaining days honorably by carrying us into the western sunset.

By way of some background, I should tell you that I am an organized person—or at least I *used* to be. Once upon a time, I took great pride in having an alphabetically arranged spice rack and an underwear drawer where tops and bottoms not only came from the same decade, but were color-matched. I'm also a person with the ability to pack a three-room grouping of furniture into the front compartment of a Volkswagen Beetle without removing the bun feet. Other people are born with all kinds of other abilities. Some of my friends are piano virtuosos, or mathematical geniuses, while yet others have wonderful singing voices. Me? I get to be a world-class furniture swamper while my friends get laid by rock stars.

In any case, that's the hand I've been dealt, so I packed and packed and packed, realizing that we would only have the trailer, a small rental truck and our Suburban to get all of our belongings across the country. I weighed every box that went into the trailer. I made sure it was balanced from front-to-back and side-to-side, with most of the weight over the tongue of the trailer hitch. Unfortunately, when we got down to the last precious few hours, it was revealed to me by my husband, the astronomer, how the pecking order of astronomers works. To wit: *This is a telescope. Despite the fact that it has not been out of its box since 1973, as an instrument of science it is of MUCH greater value than your grandma's heirloom dinnerware. Therefore, instruments of science will be loaded aboard the rental truck with the cushioned air-ride system, and your crap will be relegated to the trailer.*

The evening before our departure, I was slouched in an exhausted heap in the corner of our living room. My pupils were dilated and my pulse erratic, but we were almost ready to go. A small mountain of valuables (read: *his* stuff) remained to be loaded into the gas-guzzling truck; the trailer was locked and loaded.

We drove north and made it all the way to the Florida Panhandle before disaster struck. The driver of an eighteen-wheeler, apparently ticked off that Jack had taken too long to overtake someone in the slow lane, gave us a little "kiss" with his front bumper. That nudge sent us fishtailing along Interstate 10, where the draft from a second eighteen-wheeler finished what the first one had started. As my man tried to straighten the trailer, he drifted over to the edge of the pavement. And as soon as the trailer's wheels hit the shoulder, the ball on the trailer hitch popped off and the front end nose-dived into the gravel.

Horrified, we watched as our trailer flipped end-over-end no fewer than five times. It eventually came to a stop in the center of a jigsaw puzzle of shattered picture-frame glass. Fortunately for us, the Suburban (and its passengers) survived with all wheels firmly on the ground.

Shaken, I sat in rare silence beside Interstate 10 while Jack tried to cheer me up. He assured me that he would rent a U-Haul trailer and get us back underway in no time flat. Keep a stiff upper lip, old gal, and all of that. It was easy for him to say—it wasn't his underwear that decorated the palmettos along the roadside. (Mismatched underwear at that!)

After filing a police accident report, we were astounded to learn that we were not only responsible for paying for our own roadside cleanup, but we had to find somebody to do it. Mercifully, the state trooper who attended our scene called in a crew with a portable dumpster and enough shovels to dispatch the remains of a Hell's Gate Canyon rockslide. Turns out the crew he called in were a group of Florida prison inmates. I can assure you that their orange jumpsuits were a real eye-catcher!

The police officer then excused himself, stepped behind some bushes, and reappeared a couple of minutes later dressed in civilian clothing. Together we sorted what could be salvaged from what couldn't, and packed up the new U-Haul trailer. Among the missing items was my jewelry box (anybody check the pockets of those orange jumpsuits?), which in addition to jewelry contained souvenir bullets for every gun I'd been trained to use in Florida. The police officer told us he could return with a metal detector on his day off to search for items that might have landed in the long grass. But I was worried that, instead of rhinestones, he might find either mismatched granny underwear or a heap of bullet casings, so I declined.

Incredibly, three hours later we were underway again.

We got as far as El Paso before our next major problem. As we were leaving the interstate to stop at a rest area, we felt the U-Haul trailer suddenly slump. Upon checking it, we discovered that the trailer tongue was mere inches from the pavement. By this time my tongue was mere inches from the pavement, too! Jack discovered that an old weld had broken and the trailer was close to breaking in half. We again found ourselves on the phone to U-Haul. After an animated telephone conversation, a two-hour delay, and another complete repack into Trailer Number Three, we were once again driving west.

When we finally reached Tucson, I promised myself that I would never again have an "adventure in moving." The next home I move to will be a retirement home, followed by a rest home, and finally a funeral home. And I'm not using a trailer to get to any of them!

Alice Newton and her husband Jack are bed-and-breakfast operators from Osoyoos, BC. They spend their winters in the Chiricahua Mountains of southeastern Arizona where Alice happily hunts for pottery sherds in the high desert, while astronomer Jack studies the cosmos in search of supernovae. This is Alice's first published work.

Charming

An oxymoron if there ever was one.

By Stuart Reininger

The trip hadn't begun well. The boat to be delivered from its summer haunts in the Chesapeake Bay area to its winter playground in Tortola was a bulbous and ugly sloop of a type preferred by charter companies for its "apartment-like" amenities. Little thought had been given to its seafaring qualities.

Charming was something of an oxymoron to us. We had yanked it from the placid waters of a coastal estuary, for which it had been designed, and taken into the tumultuous North Atlantic. It protested vehemently from the start. Upon its first encounter with offshore seas it reared up in shock, then began to roll sickeningly, plunging abruptly into wave troughs as if it took every one as a personal affront. It was enough to make even a veteran salty dog sick to his stomach.

Tim, Carl and I had delivered plenty of boats together and we agreed that *Charming* was a breed unto itself. We wondered how it would act when confronted with real weather.

The answer came four days out of Annapolis. It was the kind of front—violent winds and steep seas—that is common in the Atlantic at that time of year. It was nothing that a well-found boat couldn't have handled with impunity. But *Charming* was a different matter.

The wind began blowing from the southeast, which was the direction we needed to go. A sailboat, of course, can't sail directly into the wind. The trick is to point the boat as close to the preferred course as possible. A good boat will lean into it, take the bit in its teeth, so to speak, and happily plow along. Not *Charming*. As soon as the first gusts of what I expected would be a moderate gale struck, it flopped onto its side like a mistreated puppy.

The boat's behavior wasn't completely unexpected. *Charming* was designed to perform in gentle breezes. It carried a lot of sail on a veritable skyscraper of a mast to take full advantage of those breezes. Unfortunately, the wind was far from gentle and was increasing in force by the moment. The sky took on a purplish-black hue and the seas became steeper.

We needed to "reef" *Charming*'s sails to improve stability and prevent damage to her hardware during the blow. In doing so, we also hoped to straighten her up to a more respectable profile. We began reefing—first the jib, which is the sail in front—by "roller-reefing" it around the forestay, the cable that runs from the top of the mast to the boat's bow.

But rolling the jib partway wasn't enough. As the day wore on, white-capped seas began pounding us. The wind was strengthening and the boat still wouldn't straighten up, much less sail anywhere close to where we needed to go. The mainsail eventually had to be partially lowered, which meant the only course *Charming* would obey was straight downwind, the direction we had come from.

That wouldn't do. It seemed the only option was to completely lower the mainsail and wait out the storm.

I had realized all along that lowering the mainsail on that monstrosity of a mast would be unpleasant, which is probably why I had waited a bit longer than prudent. Carl took the wheel while Tim and I strapped on safety harnesses. We crawled precariously over the cabin top, grabbed the mast for support, and struggled to our feet. The wind pinned the boat nearly on its side. Only our harnesses and white-knuckled grips on the mast kept us from sliding overboard.

"No sense just reefing it," I hollered into Tim's ear over the shrieks of wind and pounding seas. "We may as well bring the whole sail down." Tim nodded assent. The gale had become too intense to keep any mainsail aloft. The small part of the exposed jib would be sufficient to steady the boat until the weather improved.

I eased the halyard. We pulled hard and the sail inched down, flapping and thundering madly. I could see that it would be just in time; the mast was starting to vibrate like a palsied body part from the sail flogging against it.

That's when the sail jammed.

A stab of fear shot through me. I looked up at the shroud-like mainsail and felt a portent of doom.

The only thing left to do was to try and pull it in by hand. Tim and I grabbed folds of canvas and yanked until we left streaks of blood and a fingernail sticking to the fabric. The sail wouldn't budge.

A massive wall of water from an unseen wave sluiced over us. Tim and I retreated, crawling back to the cockpit as *Charming*'s decks buckled from the torsion of a thousand square feet of canvas flaying itself to death. We needed to free the boat from the sea's grip before it started coming apart. I yanked the wheel around and steered downwind.

Seconds later, the cries of tortured canvas were replaced by the roaring of seas crashing alongside as *Charming* galloped due west. The accursed mainsail, a white angel of death in the blackness, was now cheerfully driving us to our doom. A deviation of two or three degrees from running dead downwind sent waves crashing aboard and threatened a ship-sinking broach. It felt like we were aboard an eighteen-wheeler with a jammed accelerator careening down a narrow mountain road. We couldn't change course; the boat was officially out of control.

I dragged out the chart. There, a hundred and ten miles due west of our position, were the outlying shoals of Cape Hatteras. We were tearing along at almost nine knots. I didn't want to do the math. Nevertheless, I knew that if conditions remained the same, we'd hit the shoals in a little more than ten hours. The three of us huddled in the cockpit and prayed that the gale would blow itself out before we were driven onto the shoals.

Three hours later *Charming* climbed the back of the monster sea and nosedived into a trough with a shuddering crash. The bow rose like a breaching submarine and slammed down again. Seconds later, the mainsail broke free and poured down the mast. Fabric covered the cabin top and folds of canvas slid overboard, streaming to leeward.

Without the mainsail *Charming* sloughed broadside to the heavy seas. But at least with no canvas aloft it rode a little easier. The small sail area of the reefed jib held the boat steady. The bow rose and fell as the waves passed under the hull, but the seas did not wash overboard. We had "hove-to" and were now drifting toward the shoals off Hatteras rather than blindly charging at them. It was only a temporary reprieve, but at that point I would have accepted anything. The three of us scrambled on deck, hauled in the mainsail, and tied it off.

Daylight brought a flawless, sun-scorched blue sky, but *Charming* continued to pitch sharply between the troughs of the steep windblown seas. Blinding shafts of sunlight reflected through the white-flecked spume. We were drifting helplessly and would continue to do so until the weather abated enough for us to raise some sail and attempt to claw ourselves away from our collision course with the shoals. I didn't know exactly how far we had drifted overnight, but in my imagination I could already hear the crashing of seas breaking over rocks. We either needed the weather to ease or the wind to change.

As if in answer to a prayer, the wind moved to the north. We were still drifting, but not directly toward Hatteras. We had been granted some time. Things were looking up.

That afternoon, *Charming* rose yet again to meet a steep breaking wave. The bow crashed down and the forestay went momentarily slack as the mast whiplashed. As the bow rose again, the cable re-tensioned hard and we heard a loud *snap!* The stay parted and the jib instantaneously transformed into tendrils of streaming canvas. The now-unsupported mast swayed like a sapling in a breeze. Cracks formed where it was stepped through the deck. The useless thing was going to fall down. We were about to be dismasted, and if the deck buckling around the base of the mast was any indication, it was going to take part of the deck with it.

Again we turned downwind. With the pressure of the wind astern, the mast wasn't swaying as much and the backstay— the cable from the top of the mast to the stern of the boat—was managing to take the strain, steadying the mast and holding it in place. With the wind veering to the north, we weren't steamrolling toward the coast anymore.

As the day wore on, the winds and seas finally began to abate. By late afternoon, we were cruising south and were again on course in the prevailing northeast trades. We had managed to tie a rope to the end of the broken forestay and wrap it around the anchor winch, thus stabilizing the mast. We were even able to hoist a small amount of mainsail.

Carl, Tim and I congratulated each other on the exemplary way we had pulled things together. We promised ourselves that we would never again attempt to deliver a vessel so obviously unsuited to large seas. In another few days we would be in Tortola, collect a well-earned check, and get off that horribly misnamed boat. We were feeling good.

Then the whale showed up.

Now, I've seen plenty of whales over the years. Typically they appear at the water's surface where they spout or sound, thus entertaining us and breaking the tedium of the trip. Then they go on their way and we go ours. This creature, however, seemed to have a darkly humorous streak. It appeared on our port side about thirty yards off—a little too close for comfort in my opinion. The whale was roughly the same size as the fifty-foot *Charming*. It surveyed us with a dinner-plate-sized orb. Then it submerged, only to reappear a few minutes later to starboard, gazing at us with its other eye. It did this three or four times, each time passing beneath the boat. Then, during one pass, we heard a loud *thump!*

Charming turned into the seas and began hobby-horsing into the passing waves. It refused to answer the helm. The steering wheel wouldn't budge an inch—it was jammed.

The whale disappeared.

We spent the night drifting gently in the trade winds that should have been speeding us toward Tortola. By midday we confirmed what I had already suspected: our rudder was inoperable. We would later learn that its two-and-a-half-inch stainless steel shaft was bent at a ninety-degree angle to the hull, courtesy of the curious whale.

There was nothing we could do but call for assistance. The next day, after numerous attempts, a 327-foot Coast Guard cutter named the *Taney* took us in tow. The *Taney* was built in 1936 and was a survivor of the 1941 Pearl Harbor bombing. She was on her way to Baltimore, where she was to be decommissioned and put on display at a ship museum in Baltimore's inner harbor. She remains there today. We were her last "case," or rescue.

A few miles off Chesapeake Bay, the *Taney* transferred us to an eighty-three-foot Coast Guard vessel, which towed us to where we had begun our trip a week earlier.

As the two cutters were switching lines, a cheer erupted and sailors rushed aft. There, behind us, a whale had just breeched. And there, again, was that dinner-plate-sized orb gazing at us. I swear it winked at me.

Stuart Reininger spent upwards of thirty years as a professional sailor, charter and delivery captain. He decided to become a writer after discovering that writers rarely lose fingernails, sleep in cold, wet bunks, or live in constant fear of drowning. Unfortunately, after discovering that his income as a writer was insufficient to support his lifestyle, he continues to go to sea. His award-winning story "Pidge Rules the Roost" appeared in the Summit Studios anthology Never Trust a Smiling Bear.

What's in a Name?

It's enough to make a grown woman cry.

By Karen Paquin

What's in a name, Shakespeare? A rose by any other name might still be a rose, but the name itself can sure stink.

I was born Karen Regina Jamiel in Detroit, Michigan, where, although there's a large Arab American population, no one ever pronounced my Lebanese last name correctly. It's Jamie with an *l* at the end. "Jamie-elle." Seems easy enough, right? That's even the Americanized version of it. When my grandparents arrived from Beirut in the early 1900s, their last name went from the Arabic "Sh-mile," with an almost *z*-sounding *s*, to Jamiel. Welcome to America. Here's your new name.

What I generally heard when people tried to pronounce my last name was "Ja-meel." For the first ten years of my life, I was Karen Regina Ja-meel.

"No," I would say. "It's Jamie-elle."

To no avail. Then they would tell me that I didn't look Lebanese. Pardon me for being born with blond hair and green eyes.

It wasn't just my last name that was butchered, though. Whenever I was in trouble, my own mother would squish together my first and middle names. This created the vile combination of "Karie-Gene." When I heard that, I didn't run and hide just because I was going to get a whooping; I did it to get away from the sound of my name being mutilated. I like my first name, and even though I never liked Regina, Gene was even worse.

Plus, while visiting my oldest brother in North Dakota when I was about eight or nine, I learned how Canadians said my middle name. What I had always pronounced "Re-geen-ah" became "Re-ji-nah" north of the border. Even I knew what that rhymed with. No thanks.

If those wretched mispronunciations—Karie Gene, Re-ji-nah, and Ja-meel—weren't bad enough, when I was ten my parents decided we were moving to Colorado. Funny thing about Colorado: they have a large Latino population. Suddenly, I became Karen Regina Hammiel. Yes, they gave my Lebanese name a Mexican slant. So, even though with blond hair and green eyes I didn't look Lebanese, I could apparently pass for a Latina.

Longing to leave Hammiel as far behind as possible, the next stop for me was California. Finally out from under my family's wing, I grew into my own person and explored all kinds of new things. What's the first thing I did? Changed my name, of course. Anything had to be better than Karen Regina Jamiel—Jamie-elle, Ja-meel, Karie Gene, Hammiel.

I chose, for my new California name, Ayoub.

What the...?

It was my grandmother's maiden name on my father's side. I saw it once on my dad's birth certificate when I was a kid and it just struck a chord with me. It sounded right.

Maybe it's not the simplest name in the world, but how could anybody not know how to say that name when they looked at it? It's "you" with an *a* at the front and a *b* at the back. Long *a* sound, followed by "youb." A-yube. It has two syllables, not the four that many people attempted. I am sure there were times when my face contorted significantly as I listened to the destruction of my new name. Some even added random letters to it. Usually, they'd stick an *r* in it somewhere. Never the same place twice. Getting sales calls was quite painful. One guy, from the *Los Angeles Times* kept calling me Miss Ayourby—"A-your-*b*"—then wondered why I didn't want a subscription after he'd finished his pitch.

Eventually, I landed a job in New York, so I jetted off to the East Coast, where I met my husband to be. After two and a half years in the city that never sleeps, we decided that we needed a nap. So we migrated north to Providence, Rhode Island, and got married. To make the Name Game easier on me—and on any children we might have—I decided to take his last name. This was my chance to drop my horrible middle name, too. Now I was just Karen Paquin.

Life was good for about five years. Karen Paquin, long *a*. "Pay-kwin." Some people said "Pa-kwin" with a short *a*, like in the word cat. But it didn't really bother me—not like Ja-meel, A-your-*b*, or any of those other names had.

While I was enjoying life as Karen Paquin, my husband got his doctorate and accepted a job offer in Quebec, Canada. Did I mention that my newest last name, Paquin, is actually French-Canadian? Not my husband; just his name. Everyone warned me that when we crossed the border, I would no longer be Karen Paquin, but rather Karen "Pa-kaah." Okay, honestly, I can't even spell it the way French Canadians pronounce it. What I can tell you is that it sounds like the word comes out their noses when they say it. It's like magic. "Karen" out of the mouth, followed by "Pa-kaah" out of the nose. For months after our arrival in Quebec, I would catch myself staring at people's noses as if I would actually see letters falling out as they said my newest last name. I started carrying little packs of facial tissue with me and offering them to people so they could wipe away all those silent vowels and consonants after they said my new last name—"Pa-kaah" out the nose. The true joy, though, was seeing the way those same noses crinkled and nostrils flared when I told them "how we say it in the States." "Pay-kwin."

One woman replied, "Oh, that's really rather vulgar, isn't it?"

Really? I thought. *Canada has a city whose name rhymes with vagina, yet 'Pay-kwin' is vulgar?*

Thank goodness I had dropped "Re-geen-a" before I moved to Canada or I'd really be name-challenged: "Karen Re-ji-nah Pa-kaah" out the nose.

But wait. There's more. The provincial government of Quebec doesn't recognize Paquin as my last name. They consider it an alias. My official name in Quebec is Karen Jamiel. So, we've come full circle, except that the French-speaking people of Quebec pronounce Jamiel like a combination of the Arabic and American versions, so it becomes "Sha-mee-all."

This is where I let out a tiny scream. Not only did my plan to simplify my name not work, but at the moment I have a minimum of three names. Because I am American, I still have regular dealings with my home country, where I am "Karen Pay-kwin." At work and at school in Quebec, I am "Karen Pa-kaah" out the nose. And as far as the Quebec government is concerned, I am Karen "Sha-mee-all."

It's hard to keep them straight. Three identities and no prescribed drugs to help me sort them out, or to keep them in their proper places. I have more names than a spy, but none of the amenities that go with it—no secret missions, not even a Swiss bank account.

What is in a name? It sure isn't a rose. And no matter how I might try to deny my name, it's become an adventure that changes with every place I go.

Thanks, Shakespeare.

Karen Paquin's name has created adventure everywhere she's lived and traveled. She's a writer with a passion for Scandinavia, Norse Mythology and the Viking Age, including Viking Age England. Her first novel, which came out this year, is titled The Son of Nine Sisters *(released under her pen name Karen P. Foster). You can read more of her work on her blog, "The Wonder of Runes" (www.ireadrunes. blogspot.com), or at her website www.jerainstitute.com.*

Leave 'Em at Home

There is no bravery without an original fear to conquer.

By Maureen Magee

"I wish I could travel like you—you're *so* adventurous!"

I am certainly not the only solo traveler who has heard a variation on this theme, and it always makes me feel like an imposter. I am not adventurous; adventurers climb Mount Everest without oxygen or walk across Africa—that sort of thing. I travel on a shoestring budget and without an itinerary—that's all.

But to the majority of my friends and acquaintances who travel in pre-planned, deeply detailed five-star luxury, I am an Adventurous Woman.

So when my best (and most conservative) friend pleaded to accompany me on a trip, I ignored my own good-sense antennae, which were vibrating wildly, and succumbed to her enthusiasm.

Sue-Lynn had grown up in a restrictive culture and had come to Canada as a teenager. Even into her forties, she was what one might call a "good girl" and strove earnestly to follow her parents' guidelines. In terms of travel she had become accustomed to pampered tours and the swankest of hotels. I figured that strapping her into a backpack and rolling her into a hostel bunk would be a tad heavy-handed, so I decided on a compromise. I suggested that we downgrade her style of travel by a couple of stars, upgrade mine a whole heck of a lot, and ease her into the adventure she craved. I just hoped it wouldn't bore me to tears.

Well, I must say, I wasn't bored. I was too occupied with being bloody astounded to be bored. This is what I learned:

1. Compromise is vastly overrated.
2. "Adventure" is a relative term.
3. You never truly know your friends until you travel with them, and
4. If you want to keep them as friends, leave 'em at home.

We settled on a one-week stay at a three-star Mexican resort, and arranged to meet at the airport.

I found Sue-Lynn at the check-in counter, struggling with two massive suitcases and a bulging tote bag. For a woman who doesn't place much emphasis on fashion, she seemed to have suddenly morphed into a clotheshorse.

"We're only spending a week at the beach," I spluttered. "How many outfits do you need?"

"It's not all clothes," Sue-Lynn replied indignantly. "You can't pack dishes and a kettle without your bags getting bulky!"

Well, of course you can't. I knew that. And although I didn't want us to get off to a bad start, I felt the need to inquire why the kettle and dishes couldn't have stayed at home.

She blinked at me, stunned. "I always take them."

Her tone suggested that when *I* travel, I must leave my brains at home, undoubtedly in the same drawer as the utensils.

At the hotel, Sue-Lynn's luggage burst open, happy to be relieved of the kettle, a week's supply of packaged cereals, freeze-dried snacks, soup, noodles, crackers, a double set of mugs, plates, bowls and cutlery, a carving knife, a pillow, a towel, a facecloth, one bathing suit, one skirt, two tops, and enough disinfectant to swab down half of Mazatlan.

Sue-Lynn commandeered the tabletop to arrange her kitchen. Donning a pair of rubber gloves, she replaced the hotel pillow, then peeled back the bedspread and tucked the carving knife under the pillow. Finally, after peering in every corner for bugs, she disinfected the bathroom.

Eventually the room met her satisfaction and we ventured down for lunch. I ordered a beer and, anxious to start her new life of adventure, so did Sue-Lynn.

"But you never drink!"

"I'm going to try," she replied gamely. "I'm going to try *lots* of new things on this trip."

I ordered my beer and a piña colada with extra juice. She took a hearty slug of my beer, gagged, and spit it out into a nearby planter. I pushed the piña colada toward her. After a shy sip, it was pronounced delicious. She tossed it back in one long swallow and asked for another one.

"What will we do this afternoon?" she asked enthusiastically.

"Well, I expect you might want a nap."

"NO! I feel great! Let's do something!"

We explored the hotel grounds for a few minutes and then returned to our room, where Sue-Lynn came to terms with her first piña colada.

"I think I need to lie down for a few minutes…."

At 2:30, I tried to rouse her. At 3:30, she was still snoring. At 4:30, a cold washcloth on the face de-stupefied her, and we agreed that future adventures would not include alcohol.

That evening, it took a fair amount of persuasion and a detailed description of my Wen-Do self-defense techniques to convince Sue-Lynn that it was quite safe for us to wander through town on our own and find dinner. It was a lengthy process. Restaurant staff were grilled regarding ingredients. ("No ONIONS! No GARLIC!") Floors, cutlery, and toilets were inspected. Only one establishment passed muster that evening—its cleanliness upstaged only by a decided lack of Mexican ambiance. A Chicago Blackhawks game played on the television; *New York, New York* blared from the stereo.

Back at the hotel, Sue-Lynn and I came to a Mexican standoff over open windows.

"Burglars!" she said, a worried look on her face.

"We're five floors up," I countered. "No burglars are going to climb five floors of balconies." The invigorating fragrance of the tropics and the lullaby of the waves called to me from the other side of the glass.

"How do you know about Mexican thieves?" Sue-Lynn argued. And then she clinched the matter: "I never have a window open, even at home. There are night germs that will come in."

Defeated, I turned on the air conditioner. And so ended Day One.

Day Two's shopping trip was cut short when sunblock leached into Sue-Lynn's eyes. She returned to the room to sleep away the afternoon while I swam, sunned myself, and waited for her recovery.

We did not eat together that evening. The previous night, Sue-Lynn had accused me of not leaving a big enough tip; she was convinced that all the Mazatlan wait staff would know this, and would spit in our food when we arrived. The very thought of Shrimp à la Saliva made her gag and dash to the bathroom. So tonight, she announced that she would stay in the room and cook some soup. I purchased a peace offering of Pepto-Bismol before happily toddling off to a rendezvous with some garlic prawns.

For a wimp, she could sure be stubborn.

Day Three's shopping trip was cut short when Sue-Lynn overheated—having gone without sunblock because of the previous day's eye incident. She decided to return to the room for another afternoon nap. I swam, sunned myself, and got my hair braided.

We did not eat together that evening, either. Sue-Lynn's stomach was still upset, and she claimed to have discovered the reason: the Pepto-Bismol had a MADE IN MEXICO label on it.

"It *tastes* different—who knows what's in it?"

I left her boiling the bottled water to brush her teeth and headed out for some tequila tippling.

It was five a.m. on Day Four when I was awakened to the sound of burbling water, crackling food wrappers, and slurped tea. I turned on the light and found Sue-Lynn stuffing herself with the remainder of her food cache. She gave me a plaintive, sheepish look and told me that she was feeling weak with hunger.

"I really need some more sleep, Sue-Lynn. Why don't you take your tea down to the pool, watch the sunrise for a bit, and then go to the restaurant? It opens at six."

"BY MYSELF?!"

"Well, yes."

"I can't eat in a restaurant by myself!"

"Why not?"

"I've never done that! I couldn't!"

By this time, I was sitting bolt upright in my bed, and whatever composure I'd been able to summon up had totally disintegrated. "Whaddya mean, you've never eaten in a restaurant by yourself? What do you do when you travel?"

"I get room service."

I sank back into my pillows in disbelief. I thought I'd known this woman, but this trip had been one neurotic surprise after another. My mouth flapped open, but words failed me.

A wide-eyed Sue-Lynn stared back, aware that she had just confessed something major, and that her totally-in-control, has-a-smart-remark-for-any-situation friend was not only speechless, but was most definitely not in control any longer.

She finally whispered, "I suppose I could..."

"Could what?" I croaked.

"Have breakfast by myself in the restaurant. You do it when you travel alone?"

"Yes, I do."

"You'll stay here, in case I get into trouble? I can call the room?"

"Yes."

With a great show of bravado, her shoulders thrown back and her head held high, Sue-Lynn left the room.

Two hours later Sue-Lynn burst into the room. She was brimming with excitement at her first solo walk along the beach, her meal, and the friendly waiter, who had undoubtedly received the tip of a lifetime. There would be no stopping Sue-Lynn now. She was en route to becoming a liberated woman.

That afternoon, with only a suggestion from me, she agreed to a donkey ride. She handed me her camera, asking me to take photos for family back home. At her first failed attempt to throw her leg over the donkey's scrawny gray back, Sue-Lynn dissolved in giggles. A small boy pushed the depressed-looking animal back into place and urged her to try again. Her giggles turned into snorts of laughter.

"I can't, I can't, I can't…"

"Yes you can, Sue-Lynn. Stop laughing and concentrate. Try this. Stand on the curb and you'll be able to get your leg up."

She made a half-hearted attempt and the snorting escalated into full-blown hysteria. A line of prospective customers had gathered behind her and were growing restless. They rolled their eyes. The small boy rolled his eyes. I swear the donkey even rolled *its* eyes.

"GET … ON … THAT … DONKEY!" I hissed through gritted teeth. The hysterics stopped abruptly. Sobered by the look in my eye, Sue-Lynn gave one final heave and, assisted by several little-boy hands on her rump, planted herself on the stoic beast.

With her feet scuffing the cobblestones, she shrieked with delight as she was paraded through town on the back of the diminutive creature.

I followed behind and dutifully snapped photos, marveling at the expanse of her emotions. She had soared from sheer terror to exultant pride in a matter of seconds. I had to admit that she hàd guts.

Having been blessed with an ability to leap into the unknown, I realized that no matter how adventurous I may seem, there is really no bravery involved without an original fear to conquer. Watching Sue-Lynn lurch and sway on that little donkey, I wondered if my level of exhilaration would ever be as intense as hers was at that moment.

It was hard to stay angry with Sue-Lynn for long. With our holiday over, and still friends despite our tribulations, we conducted a postmortem on the return flight. Although I had been in a state of perpetual testiness, Sue-Lynn complimented me on my patience. I complimented her on the courage she had showed in broadening her horizons.

And we pledged never to travel together again.

She was, of course, wildly excited about returning to Canada. And I found myself dreaming about a nice, relaxing bungee jump and primal scream.

Maureen Magee is a Calgary-based travel writer who began traveling as a five-star butterfly, flitting lightly through distant lands and cultures. While pleasant, this required financing beyond her means, and so—defying her own nature—she metamorphosed backwards into a down-and-dirty caterpillar. She now slugs her way around the world in a far less fashionable, but infinitely more enjoyable style.

Traveling Light is for Schmucks

Or how the Queen of Packing Light was humbled.

By Colleen Friesen

Smug isn't quite the right word. Righteous, perhaps? That's closer to how I was feeling as I wheeled my suitcase past the baggage carousel and straight to the Tucson exit—where I waited (and waited, and waited) for my husband Kevin to be reunited with his bloated, overstuffed bags.

I always feel sorry for the poor schmucks who overburden themselves with excessive luggage. You know, the ones who need luggage carts or porters to assist them. Whenever possible, I strive to travel with no checked luggage and the world's lightest carry-on bag. In this particular instance, my bag was so light that I could practically have picked it up with my pinkie finger. Truly, I was the Zen master of suitcase packing … the Queen of Packing Light.

Case in point: earlier that year I had traveled to Malaysia with seventeen other travel writers. After many hours in the air we checked ourselves into the Shangri-La Hotel in Kuala Lumpur. I hadn't yet discovered my perfect carry-on bag, so I was toting one small zip bag that I'd checked and which came to sit diminutively among the piles of heavy suitcases that my colleagues were toting.

"Is that *it?*" hissed a regal-looking writer from Winnipeg.

"Uh-huh." I tried to appear casual about my packing prowess.

"What do you do? Wear the same outfit twelve days in a row?"

I smiled an indulgent and beneficent smile, a smile reserved for the unenlightened.

By the third day she was shadowing me.

"Teach me how to pack," she pleaded.

I entertained myself with the memory as Kevin eventually staggered into view with his bags in tow. Seriously, how many outfits could he need for a six-day train journey into Mexico's Copper Canyon?

To be fair, my packing system does have its disadvantages. By our third day in Tucson it was downright annoying that Kevin had room for a laundry bag to separate out his dirty clothes, which he blithely stuffed into an empty corner of his mammoth suitcase.

There were other forces at work, too. I was sweating more in Arizona than in my usual Canadian habitat, which christened the clothes I had with a fragrance that I hadn't counted on. Was my memory failing me? Perhaps on that Malaysian trip my bag had been a bit bigger than I was remembering.

Still, I wouldn't have wanted to haul bags the size of Kevin's with me everywhere.

The Sierra Madre Express consists of four refurbished 1940s- and 1950s-era passenger cars. After boarding, we discovered that our room came equipped with narrow bunks on each side and a cereal-bowl-sized sink that had been cleverly clipped so that it could swing away to reveal a Barbie-and-Ken-go-camping-sized toilet. But there were bathrooms of a more regular size down the hall and, starting on the second day, I knew we would have showers in the hotels we would be staying in.

The Sonoran desert flipped past our little window like a Roadrunner cartoon as we rocked and swayed our way south from Nogales toward Mexico's Pacific coast. Kevin heaved his bags onto the left bunk; I slid my perfect silver case beneath the narrow gap on the right, between the bed and the floor. It's funny how so much virtue can be insinuated with one deft move.

Kevin and I were excited. We were finally going to make this famous train journey, which included passage through eighty-seven tunnels and over thirty-seven bridges that had taken a century to cobble together. The Society of American Travel Writers has voted the Sierra Madre Express "the world's most exciting train ride." So, while the rooms were small, we were happy to see that the bar and lounge cars weren't. We were also happy to discover that the Mexican bartender made a mean margarita.

The next morning we were treated to more blue skies and rocking rails. It was the day we would climb to eight thousand feet. I extracted my white blouse. Not everyone who packs light would choose white, but the right items can also create a myriad of outfit options.

I felt ready for anything.

The viewing car featured an open-sided platform with a railing around the perimeter, a seat in the middle, and a bar at the back. There were also two little seats tucked into the forward corners— directly behind the locomotive.

Cherie, my new "best friend forever" who had matched

me in the margarita department the night before, was sitting in one of those little front seats when Kevin and I lurched inside. Kevin leaned against the back bar while I braced myself at the rail behind Cherie. The heat and roar of the engine were mixing with the desert air and whipping through the car. We heard the train's whistle blowing. It was loud and insistent.

"Something must be on the tracks," Cherie shouted over the train's roar. She turned to grin at me.

She turned back at the exact moment the train hit the cow. Or the cow hit the train. Or, as they say, *it* hit the fan. Because that is what we had—a fine but generous spray of bovine excrement, with a few larger blobs thrown in for good measure.

Cherie leapt to her feet, her mouth a large *O*. I gazed at the lime-colored slime on her wraparound sunglasses and the truth slowly registered. It was like looking in the mirror. The simultaneous realization of this sent us both into hysteria. We gulped air and howled uproariously.

"Oh my God," she gasped. "We're shit-faced before noon!"

Later, after sealing my white outfit in a garbage bag (which in one foul instant had reduced my outfit options by about fifty percent), I contemplated some new titles for myself. Such as, *Smug Queen Humbled by Flying Cow Excrement* or *The Queen Who Loves Her Clever Husband & His Extra T-shirts*.

Mostly, I mulled over my new mantra: *Traveling Light Is for Schmucks*.

Colleen Friesen has learned her lesson. She now wears mostly black ... a nod to her Mennonite roots and how well the color travels. She both hates leaving home and loves going on trips. When she's not writing, you'll find her on the way to Somewhere Else. You can follow her adventures at: www.colleenfriesen.com/blog.

Chaos Theory

It follows him everywhere he goes.

By Brent Curry

If anyone had wandered by the small rental car parked at the South Rim of the Grand Canyon, they would have noticed a fashionably dressed corpse lying in the trunk. The body was stuffed into a black tailored suit and spilled into the passenger compartment over the folded-down back seats. Had they noticed, they might have mistaken the man for the victim of a mafia hit. But on this night in late June, the man was actually still alive.

I should know. That man was me.

When it comes to travel, I've always tended to fly by the seat of my pants. On this particular night, those pants just happened to be a pair of gabardine slacks. I'd spent the previous week on a business trip to Phoenix and had been planning to visit the Grand Canyon afterwards. Unfortunately, after arriving in Phoenix, I realized that I'd forgotten my sleeping bag. No matter. I figured that down there in the sweltering desert I would be warm enough. I had imagined flopping down in the dirt somewhere and letting the warm air envelop me like a snug duvet.

In the end, I decided to stay in my car. I had started out in the back seat, stripped down to my underwear, thinking pleasant thoughts about what the next day would bring. However, at seven thousand feet, things cool off pretty quickly. Before long, I was searching through my bags for something warmer to wear. The best I could come up with was my black suit, so I changed into that.

Had my failure to properly prepare for the sleeping arrangements on this trip been due to all the attention I'd devoted to organizing the food I would need, I suppose the oversight with the sleeping bag could have been forgiven. Sadly, though, meal planning had also left something to be desired. Namely food.

Actually, I did have an apple and a granola bar that I'd taken from the continental breakfast at my hotel in Phoenix. I'd also snatched two cans of soda—a Mountain Dew and a 7UP—from the office fridge before leaving town. The Mountain Dew went to a haggard-looking hitchhiker I'd picked up on my way out of Phoenix. I ate the apple and granola bar in the middle of the night.

I woke the next morning at five a.m., excited to enjoy a full day at the Grand Canyon. Incidentally, it also happened to be my twenty-eighth birthday.

The previous night, I had looked at some maps at the interpretive centre. While I had been hoping to do a fairly major hike that would get me deep into the canyon, I was suddenly feeling deterred by the warning signs posted everywhere. Some featured drawings of tourists hunched over on all fours with vomit spewing from their mouths. The signs warned that hikes to the bottom of the canyon should not be undertaken alone, should not be done in the summer months, and should always be spread out over a series of days. They also had a convenient grading system, showing how much food and water one should bring along when undertaking any of the posted hikes. The suggested food allowance was shown in simple drawings of water bottles and ham sandwiches. All hikes that led into the Danger Zone—the bottom quarter of the canyon—were at least six-water-bottle and eight-ham-sandwich hikes.

Even though I didn't have any ham sandwiches, I figured I'd be more than able to tackle one of the three-water-bottle and four-ham-sandwich hikes. After all, I did have a can of 7UP, a large hydration pack, and a naive optimism that's characteristic of my generation.

After a quick change out of my suit, I began my decent into the canyon. The view at dawn was breathtaking. I jogged along, giddy with excitement and feeling that there was no place that I would rather be than right there at that moment.

On the way down I came to a junction, and a sign that presented a hiking route leading from the South Rim of the canyon all the way to the North Rim. The distance was listed at 24 miles. I immediately began to run through some mental calculations. I knew that the nearly one-mile drop down to the bottom of the canyon at 2,400 feet, and the subsequent climb of over a mile to the top of the North Rim at 8,000 feet, made my comparison of the route to a standard marathon tenuous at best. But it was too late. Danger Zone be damned! The adrenaline was already coursing through my veins and I was just too excited not to try the route.

My plan was to jog down most of the trail to the bottom of the canyon and then hike at a relaxed pace up the other side. This plan was not like some other plans I had merely imagined—but not quite fully fleshed out—such as plans involving the enjoyment of delicious food and comfortable bedding on hikes. No. This was one plan I made in earnest and executed to perfection. Believe it or not, by around 12:30 in the afternoon I had climbed my way up and over the North Rim of the canyon. I was a little tired, but in much better form than I feared I might be.

It would seem appropriate at this point to describe some details of the hike itself. The scenery, after all, was magnificent. I encountered a Grand Canyon rattlesnake along the way, as well as some deer and dozens of lizards. But here's the thing: my plan hadn't been complete. My triumphant ascent of the North Rim had one tragic flaw. Although the distance across the canyon from north to south is only about ten miles as the crow flies, if you want to drive, it takes about five hours to cover the 220 miles by road. I still needed to get back to my rental car!

It was not that I hadn't thought about this. It's just that, up until that moment, I had simply viewed it as a problem I would deal with when I got there. I had heard rumors of a shuttle bus. However, I soon learned that there was only one shuttle every day, and it had left at 7:30 that morning.

So I would have to hitchhike.

As Grand Canyon National Park is such a popular destination for travelers of all stripes, I hadn't expected much trouble getting a ride. After an hour of waiting under a blazing sun—with only a few short rides to show for my efforts—I began to wonder if I had made a mistake.

At one point, an Austrian fellow named Manfred walked past me and said he'd been walking all the way from the lodge at the North Rim. He was trying to hitchhike out to his car about nineteen miles up the road. When he made it out to his car, he was going to drive to the South Rim, so he suggested that I wait for him there if I managed to get a ride before he did.

Fortunately, that happened about fifteen minutes later. And it was all the better because I was able to coax the family who had picked me up to stop for my Austrian friend as well. It was a tight squeeze, but they found a place for Manfred to sit.

When we arrived at his rental car, we climbed in and started our drive toward the South Rim. An hour later, we stopped at a tiny truck stop to get something to drink. I had noticed the gas gauge was getting close to empty, and I had expected we would fill up before leaving. When it looked like we were going to leave with a nearly empty tank, I suggested to Manfred that we should fill up. He scoffed at the idea, claiming that we still had a good fifty miles in the tank.

"Gas will only get cheaper the further south we go," he said.

Given that we were in the middle of the desert, I thought it was probable—if not likely—that we would not hit another town for fifty miles. But I kept that concern to myself.

Fifty miles later, we were cheering and high-fiving each other as we drove into a little cluster of four buildings known as "The Gap." Our cost-saving stunt had only saved us a penny on a gallon of gas, but we didn't care—we were just relieved to have made it. But our relief soon turned to dismay as we noticed the caution tape strung across the pumps. Apparently the pumps were dry and the next gas station was thirty miles up the road. Our gas gauge read EMPTY, so it wasn't with much optimism that we set off toward the next village. Thankfully, the route had more downhill than uphill, and we took advantage of that wherever possible by cutting the engine and coasting as far as we could. Somehow, miraculously, we made it to the next gas station, where we purchased $15 worth of gas.

From there, we drove onto the South Rim and stopped at a viewpoint to watch the sun set. Then Manfred drove me around to where I'd left my car and we bid farewell.

It was about nine p.m. when I left the car park. I was exhausted, and as I drove I took stock of all the things I had eaten that day. It wasn't a very long list. In fact, the only thing I'd eaten was an ice cream cone at the North Rim of the canyon. It's amazing what a little adrenaline can do to your appetite. (I suppose the hundred-degree temperatures might have had something to do with it, too).

Starving, I stopped at a Denny's in Flagstaff. This was not only my first chance to eat solid food, but it was also my first chance to change my clothes and clean the dust off from my hike. I hadn't realized how filthy I was until I caught sight of myself in the Denny's bathroom mirror.

By midnight I was on the road again and making progress south of Flagstaff. I was still a few hours away from Phoenix, and I was starting to lose it. I pulled into a rest stop on the highway and wasted no time in kicking off my shoes and climbing into the trunk for a nap.

I woke at three a.m. It was a little later than I had expected, but I figured I would still have ample time to make my 6:57 flight out of Phoenix.

For the first time since I had stopped, I opened the car door and was surprised to hear a beeping sound. It was a lot like that beeping sound a car makes when you've left your lights on.

Oh crap, I thought, as I noticed the beam from the headlights illuminating the field in front of me. I turned the key to see if the car would start. Alas, it would not. I had already drained too much of the battery. I looked around the desolate rest stop and found no one who could help me with a boost.

In the end I had to call 24-hour roadside assistance. There is a bit of a story there too, but suffice it to say that it took me until four a.m. to get someone on their way. The truck didn't arrive until ten minutes to five, and I was back on the highway at five a.m. sharp. Would I make my flight? With a hundred miles to go, it didn't look promising.

But luck happened to be on my side yet again, as it turned out that my flight was overbooked. I generously offered to give up my seat for a $200 airfare voucher. It wasn't a hard decision, because the airline was going to route me through Dallas and I'd be home a mere three hours later than planned. Plus, they agreed to upgrade me to first class the entire way.

When I got to Dallas, I was told that the next flight was overbooked too! So I volunteered my seat once again in exchange for a $500 airfare voucher. They must have really needed my seat!

On the last leg of my flight, I was joined by forty Mexican schoolchildren. They were a rowdy bunch, and although I didn't understand the broken Spanish of our stewardess, I could tell by the way she used the word *muchachos* while simultaneously rolling her eyes that she was losing her patience with the little banditos.

Funnily enough, I actually felt a twinge of guilt about all the hyperactive kids on the plane. When you think about it, all the mayhem was clearly my fault. Chaos follows me everywhere I go!

Brent Curry owns a business called The Bicycle Forest, *which promotes the use of bicycles and other human-powered vehicles as a viable form of transportation. He has contributed several stories to Summit Studios anthologies, including the tale of an end-to-end traverse of Prince Edward Island on a sofa-on-wheels that has since been nicknamed the "couchbike" (*Mugged by a Moose*). You can visit Brent at his company's web site: www.bikeforest.com.*

Hell No Longer on Wheels

Just when you thought it couldn't get any worse...

By Rebecca Berry

I have a confession to make: I have always wanted to own a matching set of luggage. There's just something about traveling with a color-coordinated suitcase collection that seems proper. Perhaps that's why, when the opportunity came along for me to spend three months working in the United Kingdom, I decided that it was time to make the investment. I went shopping and came away with a stylish set of luggage with a lovely floral print design.

I was leaving for England the next morning, so when I got home, I started to pack. Why somebody who has the bad habit of over-packing waited until the last minute to purchase luggage is a question that will plague me for the rest of my life.

When I arrived at the Orlando airport, I had visions of myself whisking through the departures terminal with an air of regal authority, my snazzy luggage wheeling behind. My hair would be just so, my makeup flawless, my stride strong and purposeful. All the while, onlookers would be dazzled not only with my sheer beauty, but also by my luggage. How could things go wrong with such splendid suitcases?

I hopped out of my rental car, quickly unloaded my two forty-pound suitcases and carry-on, and effortlessly slung my purse over my shoulder. I put on my sunglasses and made my way through the parking lot, hair flowing, walking with a strong step as my suitcases wheeled behind. This *was* all that I had imagined.

A few minutes into my picture-perfect departure, an issue presented itself in Parking Lot B—an issue I was unable to overlook. My matching bags seemed to be getting heavier with each passing step, almost as though I were wheeling them over a shag carpet. I had weighed the bags numerous times at home, but they now felt *much* heavier. Why was there a concentration of lactic acid building up in my thighs?

My strong stride was soon reduced to short, stuttering steps. Sweat poured from my brow, and my once free-flowing hair turned limp and damp. My makeup streamed into my left eye, leaving me with a noticeable twitch. The vision I had created for myself was quickly evaporating. Instead of a suitcase model, I now looked like a circus sideshow attraction.

When I reached ticketing, a long lineup gave me time to wipe the mascara from my cheek and attempt to re-fluff my hair. It also gave me time to give the bags a quick look. Bag Number One appeared to be in fine working order; Bag Number Two was not. At some juncture in my ten-minute walk from the car to the counter, I had lost a wheel. The other wheel, although it was still attached to the suitcase, protruded at such an awkward angle that I could not imagine it being of much use. Bag Number Two was clearly a write-off. The question I now asked myself was whether Bag Number One would pull through.

I considered my options. If I were getting picked up at London's Gatwick International, as had originally been the plan, I would not have been worried. But the family I would be living with had contacted me a couple of days before to say they couldn't make it. Instead, they gave me directions on how to navigate London's train and transit system. My journey to Oswestry—an English village adjacent to the English-Welsh border—would require me to take a train from Gatwick into London, then take the London Underground across the city, followed by two more trains to get me close to Oswestry.

Having dealt with the Underground and all of its inner workings with perfectly good luggage once before, I knew that attempting it with crippled luggage would be a mistake. As with any calamity, I needed to formulate a new plan. As the plane taxied down the runway, I tried to come up with a workable solution.

After an eight-hour flight, I was unceremoniously reunited with my luggage: luggage that I had once loved and now loathed. The floral print design seemed to be taunting me.

I found a trolley, hurled my bags onto it, and wheeled my way toward the train. Trolleys, of course, are not allowed on the train platform, which meant that my bags were going to have to pull themselves together. I had two-and-a-half working wheels between the suitcases, so I volunteered Bag Number One to piggyback Bag Number Two. I knew this would put undue stress on the wheels of the first bag, but I figured I would deal with that problem when and if the time came.

That time came very soon. By the time I had made my way down to Platform Seven, I was down to a single wheel on Bag Number One, and I sensed that it only had a few rotations left before it would also expire.

While I waited for the first train with my four assorted bags and not enough wheels, I contemplated my fate. It was nine a.m. I was jet-lagged. And I knew that I would not arrive at my final destination until at least five that night.

The train was five minutes from arriving and I was still operating on Plan A. I had to figure out Plan B ... and fast. Dragging the bags was something I was not going to avoid. Nevertheless, the Underground station needed skirting, and the only reasonable way I could imagine doing that was by doling out money for a taxi. Plan B would thus read: train, taxi, train, train.

My train appeared from around a bend. It was go time. I grabbed my luggage and started hauling it toward the track. Up to this point, the dragging of my bags had been a relatively quiet operation (other than my sour mutterings). When I started pulling them this time, however, they emitted a loud screeching sound that reminded me of dragging a heavy desk across a tile floor. Fantastic! Not only did I look like a jackass pulling these stupid bags around, but now everyone's attention would be drawn to the jackass. As the train approached, I momentarily considered pushing my bags onto the tracks. But I managed to resist the temptation. Besides, that would have been too quick and painless for them.

With my heart pumping, I reached the lip of the train door and paused there for a moment to conjure up enough strength for the final pull. Just as I was about to make the all-important yank, a very nice woman offered a helping hand. As I pulled, she pushed, and together we wrestled the damaged bags onto the train with only seconds to spare before the door slammed shut and we sped north toward London.

I squished my suitcases into a corner by the door and collapsed into a seat. Exhausted from jet lag and the three minutes of hard exertion, I shut my eyes and waited for my vital signs to recover.

When the train arrived in London, I lugged the incorrigible bags through Victoria Station in search of a trolley. Victoria Station is a very busy place. It's not the sort of place where one relishes the idea of pulling around eighty pounds of screeching luggage— especially luggage that was by now leaving a trail of black streaks in its wake.

I paid a pound for a trolley, but when I tried to lift my bags onto it, the trolley inched away. I tried again with the same result. And so began the game of "around and around she went," which made me feel like a dog chasing its tail. In hindsight, this must have looked quite funny, but at the time my anger was palpable. It was made all the worse when I noticed that passersby were gawking at me without stopping to help. This might have had something to do with the profanity I was spewing forth in liberal fashion.

My next task was to find a toilet, which turned out to be one of the easier undertakings of the day. I noticed a European-style gated toilet and walked over. I asked the nice man guarding it if I could please come in.

"No," he said.

"Why not?"

"Your luggage."

Oh, the goddamn luggage. "But you're standing behind a luggage gate. Surely I'm allowed to come in through there."

"No. You have too many bags."

"So I can't come in?"

"No."

"But I really have to go to the bathroom."

"Sorry, you have too many bags."

"Why is there a gate that clearly reads LUGGAGE, with a picture of luggage on it, if someone like myself—with luggage— is not allowed through the gate?"

"Sorry."

He wasn't sorry. I'm sure of it.

I was exasperated and angry, and my bladder ached. I again considered abandoning the bags, but knew that I was not wealthy enough to absorb such a financial loss. There was nothing to do but soldier on. I pushed the luggage cart toward a TAXI sign.

Reluctant to part with my trolley, I ignored all signs that read: NO TROLLEYS BEYOND THIS POINT. Who was going to stop me? One look at my face would have sent a pride of hungry lions running for cover.

I made it to the taxi area and was relieved to see that there were plenty from which to choose. I unloaded my bags from the out-of- bounds trolley and lurched my way toward the taxi closest to me. As I reached the door, the driver told me, "You must take taxi at front of line." Of course I must. Why would I have thought otherwise?

I was sweating by the time I reached the cab at the front of the line. And was that steam coming out of my ears? The cab driver looked at me warily, but was kind and helped me to load my amputee bags. I collapsed in the back seat and then had a forty-minute conversation about London and the Olympics.

When I arrived at Euston station, there were only a precious few minutes to spare before my train would leave. This meant that there was no time to find a trolley, and in fact, barely enough time to run with the wretched suitcases to Platform Ten. Why it could not have been Platform One, I do not know. I guess that was just the way my day was rolling.

By this time, the screeching had reached an almost deafening level. In addition to the sooty stains that my bags were depositing, I would not have been surprised to learn that sparks were being dispensed with the added speed. I no longer cared; my dignity had long since left me.

When I arrived at Platform Ten, the whistle was blowing and the conductor was yelling for everybody to get aboard. I called on an improbable and final surge of strength, and somehow I managed to hurl my luggage onto the train. However, as I soon discovered, the train was full. Many people were moving between cars searching for empty seats, which I realized left me with little hope. If seats were in such short supply, then surely I would be left standing for the next two hours. I did not have that sort of endurance. However, before I could concern myself with that small problem, I had to move my bags away from the door before the next stop. I peered around the corner and saw a luggage area—a luggage area bursting at the seams, mind you—but a luggage area nonetheless. No matter. My bags were going to join the others. With a lot of banging, kicking, pushing, more kicking, and heaving, all while using the Lord's name very much in vain, I eventually managed to add my bags to the pile.

I spotted an empty seat near the luggage pile and sat down. I had not slept in over twenty-four hours. My hair was flat and greasy, my makeup was flaking, my clothes had stretched to an unrecognizable size, and I was starving.

"Excuse me." Another passenger was trying to get my attention. "Excuse me, ma'am."

I took a deep breath and feigned a weak smile. "Yes?"

"That seat is reserved. You aren't allowed to sit there."

I sat there anyway.

Five minutes before my arrival at Chester Station, I began to organize my bags for a slightly speedier departure.

The closer we got to the station, the more people filed in behind me. Everyone was in a hurry and, unfortunately, I was at the front. The pressure was intense. But as I slowly inched my bags toward the sliding train doors, a savior appeared.

"Do you need help?"

"Yes I do, thank you."

She asked which train I was catching and, when I told her, informed me that we only had five minutes to make it. This did not really surprise me. However, learning that I had to be on the opposite side of the tracks did catch me off-guard.

When the doors opened, the stranger grabbed my carry-on (the one that still had working wheels) and leapt from the train at a full sprint. She was either making off with my computer and an extra pair of socks and underwear, or expecting me to follow her unquestioningly.

"Follow me!" she shouted.

So I kicked my bags out the train door, scattering the passengers who were waiting to board in the process. I jumped out, grabbed the handles and began to run. There was, as you have come to expect, a trail of wraith-like shrieking, black streaks, and foul language following me.

I caught up with the lady at the elevator, where I was able to take a thirty-second breather. The doors opened and we were off and running along a platform that took us across the train tracks to a second elevator. I had another thirty-second breather before the elevator doors opened. Again, the lady sprinted off. She ran alongside a train until she had reached an open door, at which point she flung my suitcase inside and waited for me to catch up. She helped me load my damaged bags. I thanked her and she said goodbye before walking off wiping her brow. I was finally on the last leg of my journey.

In the future, I've promised myself that I will never again choose suitcases based on their appearance. From now on, it's going to be functionality all the way.

Dragging crippled suitcases across London is just one example of the many travel misadventures Rebecca Berry has had. She has endured blunders on trips across Africa, Europe, North America, and the Caribbean. Rebecca has since moved from Florida back home to not-quite-as-sunny Langley, BC. She is now working towards a BA in journalism, and her world travels will resume after she has her BA in hand.

Critters in the Pool

*You never know who (or what) you're going
to encounter.*

By Doug Underhill

Over the years I've had the opportunity to observe a lot of wildlife along riverbanks. But one day in the early 1990s, when my wife Barb and I were fishing in the cold pools of the Renous River in New Brunswick, we had a very unusual encounter with a swimming deer.

We were with our friend Simon, who was fishing across the river from us. I heard a snapping sound behind me, as though someone or something had stepped on a stick. I looked over at Simon, who was changing his fly. He was standing near the mouth of a small brook and wouldn't have heard the sound due to the rushing water.

Suddenly, there came the crash of foliage as a small deer jumped from the forest on Simon's side of the river, landed on the shore, then leapt into the current with a splash. The deer swam downriver toward where Barb and I were angling.

In mere seconds it was midstream and swimming madly toward me. Then it corrected course and swam toward Barb. With her back to the deer, Barb was completely unaware of the scene unfolding behind her. I hollered at her as the deer closed the distance. She turned around just as it swam past—its hooves churning the clear water—so startlingly close that she could have reached out and touched it.

The deer continued downstream for a distance, then clambered ashore and bounded into the forest. I still tease Barb about a deer putting her out of the pool.

In hindsight, we probably shouldn't have been surprised by this encounter. Many prime angling pools are located in rural or wilderness settings, so anglers should expect to experience nature up close and personal. While fishing, unexpected guests and surprise encounters at the end of the hook are not all that uncommon.

Apart from the deer, Barb and I have been put out of pools by an approaching black bear, and on another occasion, by a large bull moose. It was while fishing at Black's Pool on New Brunswick's Northwest Miramichi that we had our moose encounter. There were several anglers there that day, so we were taking turns in the pool rotation. I happened to look across the river toward a small backwater, which is when I noticed Mr. Moose standing on the far side and looking in our direction.

A few moments later, the moose decided to cross the river. I moved out of the water and hollered to the gentleman who was working the pool that he might consider doing the same. He looked at me, wondering why I was making such a fuss. I pointed across the river.

When he turned to look, I could see fear instantly materialize on his face. He did not need to be told a second time. He scrambled as fast as he could to get out of harm's way. Safely ashore, he stood mesmerized as the bull splashed his way across the river and disappeared into the forest. I am not sure if he caught any fish that day, but I don't believe he cared. Seeing that moose at such close quarters was probably enough to make his entire trip worthwhile.

Debbie Norton of Upper Oxbow Outdoor Adventures on the Little Southwest Miramichi River in New Brunswick has a beaver story. Her husband Dale and guide Stokley Harris had taken some visiting anglers to Cleland's Pool on the Little Sou'west. After fishing for a while, Dale's client had something take. He raised his rod and the battle was on!

Debbie has all of her guides "tail" fish that are caught by clients. This means that as a fish is reeled in, the guide grabs it in front of the tail fin rather than using a net, which can injure a salmon's eyes. They practice catch and release, and they do everything they can to make sure the fish is unharmed and successfully returned to the river.

As the excitement of the catch toned down a bit, Dale and Stokley realized the sport had hooked an unusual prize. There was a beaver on the end of his line.

Stokley took off for the car. When Dale asked where he was going, Stokley replied: "To get the camera. I want to get a picture of you tailing this one!" Eventually the beaver broke free, but the group had landed a good story.

Eugene Donovan of Blackville also encountered a beaver while fishing on the Main Southwest Miramichi. While making a long cast, Donovan accidentally hooked his fly on one of the creature's front paws. It took off into the bushes—still hooked—so Donovan gave the line a good pull, hoping the hook would break off. To his surprise, he pulled the beaver back out to shore, and it was in no mood for a conversation. He eventually had to cut the line.

Donovan also has a duck story. He was a schoolteacher and had taught most of the boys in Blackville over the years. One day, he saw two of his former students floating along the Bartholomew River, which enters the Main Southwest Miramichi at Blackville. Donovan was fishing in the Main Southwest when he saw the boat, and as they got near him, one of the boys asked: "Mr. Donovan, will a duck bite you?"

"No," replied Donovan.

"Good. Then will you take this duck off our line?"

To his surprise, the boys had managed to hook a duck by the foot, and were busy keeping the line tight so that it couldn't fly away. He told them to guide the duck over to where he was fishing so that he could release it for them.

Another of Donovan's favorite stories involves a friend named Wayne Holt. Donovan says that Holt was canoeing down the Main Southwest Miramichi in the Howards area when he saw an angler fishing where an old footbridge used to be. The angler had caught a salmon and landed it. He had then laid it on shore and continued fishing.

As Holt watched, an osprey dropped down and snatched the angler's prized fish. Holt continued along in his canoe, following the osprey, and was surprised when for no apparent reason the big bird dropped the fish along the shore downriver. Holt put his canoe ashore, retrieved the salmon, and took it back to the angler, who thanked him profusely. "I never thought I'd see that fish again!" said the angler.

A fisherman named Basil Connors encountered another thief on the Miramichi. Connors had caught a fish and left it on shore, only to witness a fight break out between two mink a little while later. He was quite enjoying the scrap until he realized what they were fighting over: his fish. He ran off down the river and was able to retrieve it.

I have also heard several stories of anglers who have caught salmon, cleaned them, and laid them on shore in a small pool of water to keep them cool, only to find them missing some time later. There are two possible culprits in these instances. One is the osprey, and the other is the American eel. Both are known to steal fish right out from under an angler's nose.

Hayward Sturgeon, a lifelong warden from the Miramichi area, once recalled seeing an osprey dive down and grab a salmon with its talons. Unfortunately, once the talons are locked, it's almost impossible for the osprey to let go, regardless of what happens. In this event, the determined salmon pulled the bird underwater several times and eventually drowned it. Another time, Hayward witnessed a similar encounter, and ran to get his dip net so that he could scoop the fish and save the bird. But after going under a couple of times, the bird managed to get free.

I once had an amazing encounter with a couple of big birds at Charlie's Rock on the Little Southwest Miramichi, a Crown Reserve with a stretch of great angling water. About suppertime, I was having tea with a couple of friends before heading out to fish for the evening. We were looking downriver when we noticed two large birds in flight. One was an osprey, and the other was a mature bald eagle.

The osprey was flying above the eagle and dive-bombing it. This occurred several times, until the eagle flipped over with both talons extended and made a grab for the osprey above it. Although the osprey veered and avoided the menacing talons, the eagle continued its barrel roll while continuing to fly. I can distinctly remember that nobody said anything. We just looked at each other in amazement as if to ask, "Did you see that?!"

Bears have also been known to surprise unwitting anglers. I heard a rumor about one fellow, an American visiting from Maine, who had quite the surprise as he was walking along the shore of the Miramichi. He heard a loud thump, and as he looked up, he saw that a bear had jumped down from a tree about fifteen feet in front of him. He took off in one direction while the bear took off in the other. It was later determined that the bear was probably napping in the tree when the angler's arrival woke him up.

More surprising than seeing a bird, bear, or mink taking off with your prized catch, is getting more than you bargained for at the end of your hook. Trout are known to be voracious feeders and will sometimes attack and eat smaller trout at times. I've heard at least two stories of anglers who have been reeling in a trout, only to have a larger trout attack the original. One lucky angler even managed to land both fish at the same time.

On one trip, two anglers I know were fishing for bass on the St. Croix River, which runs along the border of New Brunswick and Maine. One of them had hooked a small bass that was between five and six inches long, and as he was reeling it in, a three- to four-pound bass appeared from nowhere and swallowed both the small bass and the hook. The fisherman had both bass on his line for a while, but eventually the larger bass got free. He did land the smaller fish and decided to release it. One can only imagine the luck of that smaller fish: two near-death experiences in a single day!

One of the oddest stories I've heard was about a fisherman from Tacoma,.Washington who was fishing for spring salmon on the Little Southwest Miramichi. He felt something take the end of his line, so he reeled it in. What he found was not a salmon or a trout, but rather a clam.

Most anglers I know will tell you that while hooking or landing a fish is always a bonus on any trip, the real motivation is just to get out into nature. There is so much to enjoy while standing at the side of a river and casting a line, not least of which are the surprise animal encounters. Indeed, sometimes these events are the ones that make the whole fishing trip memorable by providing anglers with stories to tell once they get home.

Doug Underhill is a retired English teacher and a writer/columnist. His twelve books include three poetry collections, three children's books, a humorous Miramichi Dictionary, a sports book (baseball and softball), two folklore/local history books, and Miramichi Fishing Stories: All True of Course, *from which this story was adapted. Underhill writes an online weekly fishing column and has been known to cast a few lines on both water and paper! His last book,* Salmon Country, *was short-listed for the Best Atlantic-Published Book Award in 2012. You can visit him at his web site: www.dougunderhill.com.*

All is Well

It's all fun and games until somebody's house catches on fire.

By B.A. Markus

I hadn't planned to leave my husband while getting away from it all on Canada's West Coast. It just happened that way.

If I'd planned it, I certainly would have saved enough money so that I could have afforded to rent a place. Instead, the morning after the very difficult phone conversation in which I'd called it quits with my husband Lorne, I found myself three thousand miles from home on a small island that boasted breathtaking views of the mountains and sea. It also boasted what is probably the highest per capita compost-toilets-to-population ratio in Canada, and eight hundred of the quirkiest characters you'd ever hope to meet.

But there was no bank machine.

I had two hundred dollars in my pocket and a joint bank account with a man I'd just blown off after twelve years of marriage. A man who, as well as being a partner in one of the biggest corporate law firms in Toronto, would have no qualms about withdrawing every last penny from our bank account just to teach me a lesson.

It was obvious that I could no longer afford to stay at the bed-and-breakfast I'd originally booked for the duration of my month-long getaway. A little time alone had suddenly turned into a full-fledged flight from the confines of matrimonial misery, and for the first time in twelve years I had to fend for myself.

Like I said, I hadn't planned to leave my husband. But for some reason Green Island (not its real name) has that effect on people. You just never know what's going to happen when you board the ferry that takes you from the shores of Vancouver Island across the Georgia Strait to this tiny thirty-square-kilometer island. Fortunately, as crazy and unpredictable as life gets on Green, things always seem to work out. Which is why within an hour of realizing that I was effectively homeless and almost penniless, I saw the notice on the bulletin board at the library asking if somebody on the island was interested in a house-sitting gig.

I called the number from a phone booth outside the library and was invited right over.

Jeff and Paula and their two kids lived on a quiet stretch of gravel road that rolled and dipped, offering up fleeting views of the Coast Mountains on the faraway mainland. I made the typical city person mistake and went to the front door. Jeff came out the back and ushered me in that way, up the four wooden steps and through the mudroom.

It was a comfortable, ramshackle house that smelled like a combination of homemade bread, woodsmoke and old dog. Downstairs was a big cluttered kitchen with windows that looked out on the yard, and a living room amply stocked with worn-out couches and La-Z-Boy chairs. Books, magazines, cassette tapes, and CDs were piled everywhere. Upstairs, Jeff showed me the master bedroom and the kids' rooms, all of them bursting with the detritus of family life.

"Sleep wherever you want," he said apologetically. "Sorry about the mess."

We went back down the narrow, uneven stairs to the first floor.

"Ever use a woodstove?" Jeff asked.

"Sure." I was afraid Jeff would change his mind if he discovered how little I knew about country life in general and woodstoves in particular. But he must have suspected my lack of experience because he spent a long, long time explaining in great detail how the stove worked and showing me the woodpile and the kindling and the big red fire extinguisher on the wall.

Just as he was finishing up, Paula came in. She was less than five feet tall with delicate bones, but when she shook my hand I could feel the strength and resilience that ran through her like an electric current.

"Hi." She gave me a gentle smile. "Did Jeff tell you about the dog?"

Jeff hadn't mentioned the dog, although the smell I'd noticed when I stepped in the door had led me to suspect that there was one around.

"I like dogs," I said, hoping to endear myself further. "It'll be nice to have some company on my walks."

Paula laughed. "Don't count on it. Sasha hasn't made it down the drive in months." I followed my hosts into the mudroom. Curled up in a worn wicker doggie bed behind the freezer was the family pet, a barrel-chested black lab gone gray around the eyes and snout. The old dog lifted her head when we came in and opened her eyes, but it was obvious that she was totally blind from cataracts. I could tell she was friendly from the way she wagged her tail and from the little musical whimpering sounds she made.

"She smells bad, but she's a real good dog." Paula leaned down to pat Sasha on the head. "Aren't you, old girl?" Sasha wagged her tail again and whimpered.

"Her arthritis is worse with all this rain," Jeff explained. "If this keeps up, you might have to carry her down the back steps so she can go."

"That's okay. I'm sure I'll be fine." I leaned down to give Sasha a little pat.

"Great," Jeff said. "We're leaving on Monday."

The move from the bed-and-breakfast to Jeff and Paula's house was easy. They'd left the keys to their pickup and I didn't have much stuff—just a couple of boxes of books, my clothes, and my laptop.

After I had moved in, I made myself a cup of tea and took a couple of deep breaths to try and relax. It was time to call my mother and tell her about my breakup.

I flashed back thirteen years to the day I had called her from a campground on Cape Breton Island to tell her that I was engaged to Lorne and that we planned to get married the following summer. I was nineteen and my father had already been sick for five years. Even over the phone, I could feel her relief. Her youngest and wildest daughter would now be someone else's responsibility. Lorne had everything, and she didn't have to look after me anymore.

Now I had to tell her that we were getting a divorce.

"Hi Mom, it's Eve."

"Darling, where are you?" She always asked me that question when I called from Green, like she was hoping I had come to my senses and was calling her from my cell phone in the elevator of her condo building.

"Still here. On Green Island."

"I saw the weather on the news. It looks horrible out there."

I looked out onto the yard. The rain was coming down in sheets and it was so dark at eleven a.m. that I had all the lights on. "It's not so bad."

"Is something wrong, Eve? You don't sound good." Three thousand miles away and she could still tell that something was up.

"Mom, things have changed between me and Lorne. I've realized that I don't love him anymore."

There was silence on the other end of the line.

"Mom? Are you still there?"

My mother's voice was stiff, hard. "I'm here."

"I can't pretend any longer."

"Poor Lorne."

"He didn't seem too bad when I spoke to him. He said he'd see me in court."

"He loves you so much. He must be in shock."

"He's fine." I could feel myself starting to get angry. "He's got all his friends and family around. Everyone is in Toronto."

"That's true," my mother conceded. "So when are *you* coming home?"

"That's not what I meant."

"You can stay with me as long as you want."

"I'm not coming home, mom."

"You'll have to support yourself now, you know. It won't be like it was with Lorne. He treated you like a little princess."

I heard Sasha whimpering in the mudroom. "I'm really sorry, mom, but I have to go now. The dog has to go out."

"Don't tell me you bought a dog. You don't even know how to take care of yourself."

"She's not mine," I said, hoping to calm her down. "I'm house-sitting. To save money."

But once my mom was on the worry track, it was impossible to get her off. "I don't believe you've thought this thing through properly, Eve. Just think about what you're throwing away."

I imagined our house, the car, my walk-in closet filled with clothes and shoes. And then I thought of Lorne, pictured him shoved headfirst into a dumpster, and felt an immense sense of relief.

Sasha whimpered again.

"I have to take the dog out. I think she has to go to the bathroom."

"I wish you'd come to your senses and come home. I'm sure Lorne would still take you back."

As she said it, I knew immediately that going back to Toronto was the last thing I wanted. In that moment I decided I would stay on Green and be one with the quirky people. They would be my new family.

"I'll call you soon, mom. I promise."

"Don't do anything crazy. You know how you can be."

I hung up, put on my boots and raincoat, picked up Sasha, and carried her down the back steps. The rain had eased and I could see the sky lightening through the filigreed cedar boughs. I tried to stand Sasha up, but her hind legs were useless and just slid out from under her. The ground was wet and I didn't want to lay her in the mud, so I ended up squatting down behind her and holding her back legs up with my hands. She managed to crane her neck around and look toward me with her metallic, cataract-clouded eyes. I think she appreciated what I was trying to do, but it was hard to tell.

When she had finished, I carried her back inside. I refilled her food and water bowls, but she lay back down right away. She didn't seem hungry. I went back outside to fetch kindling and logs for the fire, which I put down in the living room. As I began to ball up sheets of newspaper from a basket beside the woodstove, I reviewed Jeff's fire-lighting instructions in my mind.

I took my time constructing a teepee of kindling over the paper, and then readied a pile of bigger sticks to feed the fire when it was time for the larger logs to go in. It took a couple of matches to get the paper going, but in a few minutes the fire was burning pretty well; fat flames licked the wooden teepee, and I could feel little fingers of warmth reaching out into the room. The cheerful blaze seemed like a good omen to me, an affirmation that everything was going to work out all right after all.

I watched the flames, enjoying the warmth and the sound of the crackling wood. After about half an hour of daydreaming, it occurred to me that I should do something memorable to ritualize the end of my marriage—something I could think back on later as the official beginning of my new life. I went through a cardboard box I'd brought with me and took out a couple of photos of me and Lorne skiing at Mont Blanc the previous Christmas, plus a postcard I'd written to him a few days before New Year's and never sent, and five or six poems I'd been working on for a while but could never get right. I also added a used sanitary napkin to the pile: a bizarre gesture to some, perhaps, but in my mind the symbolism was perfect. Blood and death. Beginnings and endings. Thank God I left him before I got pregnant.

My idea was to burn everything up. To incinerate my past life and all its falsity with a purifying fire that would make space for the new me to emerge like a phoenix from the ashes. But something was missing. I needed some kind of formal prayer to ritualize and bless the moment. I was raised on Friday night blessings and synagogue-directed prayers, and I figured some well-chosen words would really help to symbolize the transition.

I scanned my hosts' bookshelves for inspiration and lucked out. There, right beside a dog-eared copy of *Slaughtering Chickens for Fun and Profit* was a more useful book: *Helpful Spells for Modern Witches* by Eagle MoonRay. I scanned the table of contents and flipped to the chapter on "Spells for Self-Protection and Security."

The book said that all I had to do was follow the four simple instructions below in order to feel an immediate sense of inner security and self-protection.

Sasha whimpered again. It was cold in the mudroom, so I lifted her out and brought her closer to the fire. With the old dog settled in front of the woodstove, I dug out my bathrobe from the suitcase. It was a voluminous purple velour affair with large sleeves and a hood: just the right accessory for a ritual of this sort. I went back to the book.

1.   Light a few candles.
2.   Call on the four directions.
3.   Say the prayer that's written in this book.
4.   Repeat the prayer until you believe it.

I found some candles in a kitchen cupboard, lit them, and placed them on the floor on both sides of me. I wasn't quite sure what the book meant by calling on the four directions, so I just turned around and at each quarter-turn called out, "North," "South," "East," and "West," in both English and French, because that seemed more inclusive. Then I faced the stove, raised one arm in a kind of I-am-evoking-the-Great-Spirit pose, and started in on the prayer.

I am a child of the universe.
She fills me with her protective spirit.
I will be safe from accidents,
Injuries, sickness and death.
All is well, all is well, all is well.

I said the prayer a couple of times until I had it memorized. Then I stoked the fire with the poker. It didn't yet look impressive enough for my purposes, so I added some more logs, opened up the flue all the way, and waited for the wood to catch. I poked the fire again, shoved in my collection of mementos—including the used feminine hygiene product—and slammed the door fast because I was afraid of getting ashes on the floor.

At first, nothing happened. I looked over at Sasha, my adopted animal companion, for inspiration. But she appeared to be asleep. I decided to keep on praying.

I am a child of the universe.
She fills me with her protective spirit.
I will be safe from accidents,
Injuries, sickness and death.
All is well, all is well, all is well.

I was swaying around the room in a witchy, emerging-goddess kind of way to get more into the mood when the edge of my bathrobe got a little too close to a candle and caught on fire.

As I was putting out the flames on my robe, the photographs, postcards, and poems finally caught fire in the woodstove. Okay, okay, I thought, I've put the fire on my robe out. I'll simply ignore the stench of singed purple velour and keep right on praying.

I took a moment to meditate on the flames that were licking up the inside of the stove. The fire was a metaphor for my own purification. It marked the necessary destruction of my past life that would allow for a new beginning, a beginning of my own creation. I imagined that by lighting that fire and saying the prayer, I was in fact incarnating the Goddess Kali, the mother of birth and death, who creates and also destroys. I swayed a little closer to the woodstove. The fire was really burning now, but strangely, the menstrual pad was still intact.

As I leaned in to get a closer look, there was a sudden blinding flash of light. The needle for the chimney thermostat—the one Jeff had told me to keep at Medium—swung wildly to the right and into the Extreme Danger zone. The inside of the stove was now a solid ball of flame. The handle on the door was too hot to touch, and I didn't know what else to do, so I just kept on praying.

I am a child of the universe.
She fills me with her protective spirit.

The stovepipe started shaking. Smoke poured out of it, and flames leapt out through the cracks on top of the stove. The thermostat needle read Nuclear Holocaust. I screamed:

I will be safe from fire, fire, FIRE!!

I grabbed the fire extinguisher with one hand, and with the other, a small, fringed couch pillow to protect my hand as I yanked open the stove door. The wall of heat almost knocked me over. There were flames everywhere. I aimed the nozzle directly into the inferno, adopted my best Bruce Willis stance and pulled the trigger. White foam shot out with an impressive *whoosh* and expanded to fill the stove completely, then billowed out the door and onto the floor. In a matter of seconds the fire was out.

The room was suddenly quiet. I watched as a mushroom cloud of fire-extinguisher carcinogens drifted languidly up from the woodstove to rest gently against the ceiling.

When I put the extinguisher down, my hands were shaking and my heart was pounding so hard it was difficult to breathe. The living room was covered in ash and the room was hazy with smoke.

"My marriage is over," I croaked. "All is well, all is well, all is well."

I was just starting to clean up the mess when I realized that at some point during the "ritual," Sasha had taken her last breath.

So my mother was right after all. Without someone to watch out for me, I was sure to do something crazy and irresponsible. It was obvious that I was incapable of looking after myself.

The smells of extinguisher fumes and recently deceased dog were too much for me. I opened some windows, took off my robe, put on my boots, and went outside. The air was better out there. The sky was clear and I could see a crescent moon peeking out from behind the clouds. I needed to walk for a while, to clear my head, but all I could think about was how stupid I'd been, how I was going to be the laughingstock of the whole island, and how I might as well beg Lorne to take me back right now because my only other option was to spend the rest of my life living with my mother.

By the time I got back to the house I'd stopped crying, but I was still feeling terrible. When I walked in the door, the phone was ringing. I tried not to look at Sasha or the mess around the woodstove, and prayed it wasn't Jeff and Paula calling to check on their house or their beloved family pet. I figured the Goddess owed me that much at least.

"Hello, Eve?" I recognized the breathy voice on the other end of the line right away. It was Isis, Green Island's resident astrologer. I'd met her a couple of times at the Gas Bar Café.

"Hi Isis. Jeff and Paula aren't here."

"I know that."

Of course she did. Everyone knew everything about everybody on Green Island. That was exactly why I had to get on the next ferry, before I could see my failure reflected on the faces of the strangers I'd been stupid enough to think would one day be my new family. Her next sentence caught me off guard.

"I was wondering if you'd like to participate in a little ritual I'm organizing."

The word "ritual" made my stomach churn. Was it possible that she already knew what I'd done in Jeff and Paula's house? Was a hidden webcam broadcasting the whole sorry affair into the Gas Bar Café? Or did her astrological powers involve some kind of psychic element?

"Ritual?" I stammered. "Ah, well, actually I'm not really familiar…."

"I'll be leading it, of course," Isis reassured me. "I just finished a Wiccan correspondence course."

"It's really nice of you to invite me," I said, and I meant it. It was just too bad that the invitation had come too late. I'd already blown any chance at making friends on Green Island.

"We're going up to Stanton Park. Elliot Dale's started developing up there and he's going to cut down a whole stand of Garry oak. I thought you'd be interested, since I heard you like to walk out there."

"I really appreciate the invitation, Isis. But I'm afraid I'll be leaving Green Island sooner than I had expected. I have to go back to Toronto."

Then I found myself telling Isis the whole story about the ritual and the inferno and Sasha dying and me being sure that everyone on the island was going to revile and despise me forever.

Isis laughed. "Are you kidding? Things are so boring around here in January that you're going to be the toast of the Gas Bar Café for weeks."

"What?"

"Listen, Eve," Isis said. "I'm sure you've noticed that pretty much everyone around here is slightly odd. Almost burning down the first place you housesit and probably causing the death of the family dog while doing a pagan ritual is kind of like your initiation into life on Green Island. It means you're just as crazy as the rest of us."

"But what about Jeff and Paula and the kids?"

"They'll be fine," Isis assured me. "Sasha's been ready to pass on for months, and Jeff would have put her down himself if he wasn't such a softie. He's a Libra rising, and you know how they are."

"Uh-huh," I said, though I had no idea what she meant. Still, I was starting to feel better. And I had noticed that pretty much everybody on Green was a little strange, albeit in a good way. That was part of what had attracted me to the island in the first place. "You really think it will be okay?"

"I guarantee it. So, can I count on you for the ritual?"

"Sure," I said. "It's for a good cause and it actually sounds like fun. Just don't let me near the matches."

Isis laughed. "I'll keep that in mind."

"One more thing," I said. "I think I know how to clean up the mess in the living room, but what should I do about Sasha?"

"What's your time, date, and place of birth?"

It seemed irrelevant to me, but I wasn't going to question the logic of someone who was starting to make me feel like I belonged on Green. "One-fifty in the afternoon on December 23, 1973. Toronto, Canada."

I heard Isis tapping away at a computer keyboard. "Very interesting," she said. "You're such a capable person." She'd obviously never spoken to my mother.

"So what should I do about Sasha?"

"I don't have to tell you that, Eve. You're a Capricorn with Taurus rising. You'll figure it out all on your own."

I wasn't feeling so sure about that when I hung up the phone, but whatever Isis saw in my chart that day must have been true, because by the time the living room was tidied up, I'd figured out what to do with the dog's body.

First, I took an old towel from the bathroom and lifted her onto it. Then I went into the mudroom and moved things around in the big freezer. It was easy enough to fit Sasha inside after that.

I was relieved that her eyes were closed and she seemed to be at peace.

I couldn't just put the towel over her head and close the freezer door without saying anything, so I decided to repeat the only prayer I knew by heart. I shortened it a bit so it made more sense.

You are a child of the universe.
She fills you with her protective spirit.
All is well, all is well, all is well.

B.A. Markus is a self-proclaimed bicoastal Canadian who wishes she could live in the heart of the BC rainforest and the urban jungle of Montreal at the same time. When she's not writing or teaching, she has a penchant for performing rituals of her own creation that usually involve setting something on fire.

Do you have a Great Story?

If you enjoyed this collection of stories and feel you have an outrageous, funny, heartwarming or inspirational tale that you would like to share, we would love to hear from you. Our only rules are that your story has some unusual, illuminating or humorous twist to it, that it's a true anecdote, and that it has something to do with travel or the Great Outdoors.

Although we already have six volumes in our travel and outdoor humor series, we are still hoping to publish more books in this genre. So if you have a great story, please send it to us. You don't have to be a professional writer. We look forward to hearing from anybody that has a great yarn to spin.

To obtain more detailed submission guidelines, please visit Summit Studios on our web site at:

www.summitstudios.biz

Please submit stories or story proposals by e-mail or snail mail to:

SUMMIT STUDIOS
80 Cardinal Cres.
Newmarket, Ontario L3Y 5Y4

E-mail: submissions@summitstudios.biz

We look forward to hearing from you.

Acknowledgements

A very special thanks to my wife, Stacey, who shares my passion for travel and the outdoors. She also shares my love for great stories. Without her unconditional support and her belief in my dream to found a publishing company, it would not have been possible to share these stories with you.

A big thanks to Curtis Foreman for his help with the copy editing and to Kirk Seton for a fantastic book design. They are both top-notch professionals.

Thanks to Doug Lindstrand for the great cover photo of the moose.

Thanks to my friends and family members who have offered their ideas, support, and critical feedback as this book has taken shape.

And finally, thanks to the many travelers who have contributed their stories to this book. Their willingness to share means that we're all a little richer.

Other Titles by Matt Jackson

Mugged by a Moose

Edited by Matt Jackson

Is a bad day spent outside really better than a good day at the office? This collection of twenty-three short stories aims to answer that question.

Humor/Travel • Softcover • 216 pages
$19.95 • ISBN 9780973467130

Canadian Bestseller

"It's like Chicken Soup for the Funny Bone."

- The Kitchener-Waterloo Record

I Sold My Gold Tooth for Gas Money

Edited by Matt Jackson

Alternately laugh, cringe and giggle as twenty-six travel writers find themselves in some bizarre and unexpected situations.

Humour/Travel – Softcover – 216 pages
$19.95 – ISBN 9780973467147

Never Trust a Smiling Bear

Edited by Matt Jackson

The fifth volume in our bestselling humour series, where thirty-one writers serve up another helping of preposterous travel and outdoor tales.

Humour/Travel – Softcover – 216 pages
$19.95 – ISBN 9780973467185

The Canada Chronicles: A Four-year Hitchhiking Odyssey

Written by Matt Jackson

Join the author on a four-year hitchhiking journey across Canada as he logs almost 30,000 kilometers, takes more than 25,000 photographs and meets hundreds of interesting characters from every corner of the country.

Adventure/Travel • Softcover
384 pages • 60 color photographs
$25.00 • ISBN 9780973467123

Canadian Bestseller and Winner of the 2005 IPPY Award for Best North American Travel Memoir!

"Jackson's humor and charm shine throughout his storytelling."
- Canadian Geographic Magazine

A Beaver is Eating My Canoe

Edited by Matt Jackson

Another collection of wacky, funny, and inspiring tales from the far side of beyond, written by twenty-five free-spirited wanderers.

Humor/Travel • Softcover • 224 pages
$19.95 • ISBN 9780973467161

A Bear Stole My Fishing Boat

Edited by Matt Jackson

Traveling is not for the timid of heart. What can go wrong often does, as twenty-six travel-hardened writers relate in this book.

Humor/Travel • Softcover • 216 pages
$19.95 • ISBN 9780973467178

About Matt Jackson

A graduate of Wilfrid Laurier's Business Administration program in Waterloo, Canada, Matt Jackson was lured away from the corporate world by the thrill of adventure journalism while still a university student. He is now an author, editor, photojournalist and professional speaker, and is the president of Summit Studios, a publishing company specializing in books about travel and the outdoors.

Matt's first book, *The Canada Chronicles: A Four-year Hitchhiking Odyssey*, is a Canadian bestseller and won the IPPY award for best North American travel memoir in 2004. He has also been featured in more than two dozen popular magazines including *Canadian Geographic, Backpacker, Explore, Canoe & Kayak,* and *BBC Wildlife*.

He currently lives with his wife Stacey in Michigan, where they spend as much time hiking and kayaking as possible.